Emotional Abuse

Emotional Abuse

The Trauma and the Treatment

Marti Tamm Loring

Jossey-Bass Publishers • San Francisco

140703

Copyright © 1994 by Jossey-Bass Inc., Publishers, 350 Sansome Street, San Francisco, California 94104.

FIRST JOSSEY-BASS EDITION PUBLISHED IN 1998
THIS BOOK WAS ORIGINALLY PUBLISHED BY LEXINGTON BOOKS

Jossey-Bass books and products are available through most bookstores. To contact Jossey-Bass directly, call (888) 378-2537, fax to (800) 605-2665, or visit our website at www.josseybass.com.

Substantial discounts on bulk quantities of Jossey-Bass books are available to corporations, professional associations, and other organizations. For details and discount information, contact the special sales department at Jossey-Bass.

For sales outside the United States, please contact your local Simon & Schuster International Office.

Manufactured in the United States of America on acid-free paper.

Library of Congress Cataloging-in-Publication Data

Loring, Marti Tamm.
    Emotional abuse : the trauma and treatment / Marti Tamm Loring.
        p.   cm.
    Originally published: New York : Lexington Books, 1994.
    Includes bibliographical references and index.
    ISBN 0-7879-4377-0 (pbk.)
    1. Psychological abuse. I. Title.
    RC569.5.P75L67   1998
    616.85'82—dc21   98-20964

FIRST EDITION

HB Printing   10 9 8 7 6 5 4 3 2 1
PB Printing   10 9 8 7 6 5 4 3 2 1

To my mother,
Esther F. Tamm

and to emotionally abused individuals
in their quest for emotional survival
and hope, and the therapists who help
with this transformation

Contents

Preface

In the ensuing chapters I use several terms in a fairly specific way. First, throughout the book I use gender-specific pronouns to identify the victims and perpetrators of emotional abuse. Thus *she* generally refers to those who are abused, and *he* usually designates the abuser. This format is utilized in numerous other works related to issues of family violence because—with the exception of children—women have been viewed as the most frequent victims of abuse (whether physical or emotional). Where abuse generated by women occurs, it often arises as a form of self-defense.

Nonetheless, gay and heterosexual men, lesbians, children, adolescents, and the elderly do become targets of emotional abuse, and studies focused on their experiences are needed as well. The use of gender pronouns here is not meant to discount their very real pain. In the Epilogue I discuss certain special aspects of the experience of emotionally abused lesbians, children, and men.

I use the term *psychosocial* to convey the ongoing blend of inner dynamics, relational connections, and social forces that shape an individual's life. My view of emotional abuse thus takes in a broad human context and assumes that for each individual the healing process flourishes or fails insofar as it is supported by significant relationships and opportunities to achieve in the community. These opportunities offer victims pathways to produce creatively and reintegrate an eroded sense of self, to form supportive relationships, and to discover the security of carving out a comfortable place in the world. This is, in essence, the journey from victim to survivor.

I use the term *emotional abuse*, rather than *psychological abuse* or *maltreatment*, in an attempt to encompass the relational and societal components of this process. Similarly, the word *violence* is used in the broad sense of causing hurt or injury, either physically or emotionally. In the first five chapters, *Victim* denotes the person who is emotionally abused; the terms *client* and *survivor* designate the abused person in the context of the model of therapy described in Chapter 6. This usage is meant to depict a movement toward surviving—a lifelong endeavor for those who have experienced emotional abuse.

Attachment is viewed as a unilateral effort on the part of the abused person to bond with another, whereas the term *connection* connotes a process providing opportunities for mutual empathy, knowledge, and responsiveness. *Disattachment*, in contrast, designates an ongoing separation process in which the client, after reintegrating her formerly fragmented self, breaks away from the emotional abuse process. By using this term I intend to emphasize that it is not realistic to expect separation from an abusive connection unless it is preceded by the achievement of certain critical steps: self-development, recognition of the abuse process, and creation of skills for building and maintaining the self-system and forming nonabusive connections. This process is quite different from that described by the term *detachment*, which connotes an immediate and complete separation. Using the latter term could create expectations that exceed the capacity of the emotionally abused client to realize them; it may result in additional feelings of failure in an already despairing individual.

It is possible that therapists and others reading this book will experience secondary trauma. Traumatic experiences from their own pasts can be triggered by reading case study excerpts, case descriptions, or even materials on development of a theory base and therapy model. The symptoms of this secondary trauma may include profound sadness and loneliness, difficulty concentrating, sleeplessness, irritability, and grief reactions. Somatic reactions like nausea and headaches are also common.

It is not unusual for an individual to become retraumatized or suffer feelings of grief when reading about issues of attachment and trauma. Usually the reader will be aware of the specific experience—such as a recent loss or a past abusive incident—that has triggered the secondary trauma. At certain times, however, the incident may lie outside consciousness.

Therapists and advocates for the abused need to remember that they, too, are vulnerable to sadness and trauma in reaction to human tragedy. Hearing about atrocities that collide with their own beliefs about fairness or wishes for security can be very upsetting. Like the trauma survivors they work with, they may experience intrusive thought and painful reactions. Exploration of the work by McCann and Pearlman (1990b) on "vicarious traumatization" may be beneficial; or they may need to discuss their feelings in a supportive environment with colleagues or in therapy.

Therapists utilize a wide range of theoretical perspectives in diagnoses and treatment. Certain components essential for the initial treatment of emotional abuse may not be part of a particular perspective. In the initial stages of treating an emotionally abused client, therefore, the therapist will need to utilize a therapeutic model that specifically addresses this type of problem. I describe such a model in Chapter 6. In later sessions other forms of therapy can be utilized.

Both therapists and lay readers should understand that the case examples used in the book are composite portraits of more than one person, and that identifying information has been changed or omitted.

Finally, individuals can recognize their own abusiveness and strive toward change. Great courage is demonstrated by emotional abuse victims who struggle to stay alive physically, emotionally, and spiritually. It is crucial that therapists and the general community reach out to help and encourage emotional abuse survivors.

Acknowledgments

Lifelong encouragement for all of my efforts is a trademark of my mother, Esther F. Tamm. Don Devis, M.S.W., was continually supportive during the writing of this book. Thanks to Roger Smith, M.S., a graduate student at GSU who delved into research and theory to assist with the book. Pam Borden spent many hours as an undergraduate at Georgia State University (GSU) assisting with this effort. Margaret Zusky, editor at Lexington Books, is my mentor in the art of developing my own voice in the book. Anne Love, M.S.W., was coach par excellence. The support of Claire Blackwell, M.Div., was invaluable.

I also wish to express my appreciation to Kathleen O'Malley, who believes in my writing, and send my particular gratitude to book team members Pam Borden, Roger Smith, M.S., Jennifer Keats, Christine Frost, Benita Quakenbush, Cynthia Lamutt, Marcia Wiggins, and Anna Marie Dickerson. Students Virginia Jordan Diehl, R.N., and Pat Fulton shared encouragement and ideas during revisions.

Individuals from the Stone Center at Wellesley College were very helpful; Jann Sulzen made certain that I had access to the important work on connections from the center. For their encouragement, I send my thanks to Dr. Judith V. Jordan, Dr. Sandy Bloom, Dr. Christine Courtois, Dr. Jean Baker Miller, Dr. Kathy Bruss, and Dr. Marolyn Wells.

The research analysis described in Chapter 2 was conducted by Dr. David L. Meyers and myself. Help from Angela D. Hagen was appreciated. Additional support was provided by Milton Picard, Drew Findling, Howard Gold, Laine S. Walker, and Charlie

Corbin, M.S.W. My friend and researcher par excellence, Dr. Brian Powell, is wonderful.

Special appreciation is due to Oprah Winfrey. A woman calling Atlanta's annual December Depression Hotline said that before she learned about emotional abuse by watching other victims on Oprah Winfrey's program, she had been convinced she was crazy. Oprah's encouragement to share knowledge about important aspects of human relations is a significant service in contemporary American life.

My own thanks are also due to producer/director Jocelyn Dorsey, for her vision and support, and to Rhonda Aniton and Monica Glass at WSB-TV in Atlanta for their caring and ongoing efforts to educate the community in mental health areas. Nancy Stafford, public relations specialist at GSU, has also contributed to the public's knowledge of interpersonal violence. Dr. Louise Bill shared valuable contributions to this book and to the field of family violence. Thanks also to Professor Kiki Thomas, Dr. David Niles, E. Dean Moore, M.S., Stacy Lange, Dixie Richardson, Julia M. Campbell, Helen S. Akram, and Lola Glasper. Thanks to students at Shorter College, especially Beverly Mason.

My shadow (who followed me from room to room), the blind cocker spaniel, Buffi, who saw with her heart; her brother, Corki, with his tennis ball gripped firmly in his jaws; and Noelle the cocker spaniel were an ongoing source of joy and companionship during the long hours of writing and revisions. A squirrel named Ichabod, who was medically treated and recovered after being smashed by a car, was a visible symbol of healing. He came to perch on the windowsill many times as the book was revised.

Most of all, I appreciate the help of victims and abusers who shared information about the traumatic and tragic components of their emotional abuse. And thanks to President Bill Clinton whose Thanksgiving Day visit to a shelter for abused women in 1993 symbolized the need for universal concern about family violence.

Emotional Abuse

1

Emotional Abuse

An Overview

Emotional abuse is an ongoing process in which one individual systematically diminishes and destroys the inner self of another. The essential ideas, feelings, perceptions, and personality characteristics of the victim are constantly belittled. Eventually the victim begins to experience these aspects of the self as seriously eroded or absent. Ginny, an emotionally abused thirty-two-year-old attorney, describes this phenomenon:

> After my husband has called me "utterly worthless" and "boring," and ignored me for a few days, I begin to feel very small and unimportant. Sometimes I can't remember who I am. I've lost myself somewhere. What are my real characteristics? Who is the neat person I once thought I was? It's like losing your dog. Once I even fantasized advertising in the newspaper for someone to find me, as if I were a lost dog.

Although emotional abuse is a widespread form of violence, it is rarely recognized by its victims. Many are convinced that they are at fault and thus do not perceive themselves as abused. When they seek out a therapist it is usually to deal with symptoms like suicidal ideation, intrusive thoughts, terrified clinging behavior, and pervasive feelings of confusion and unreality. Even when victims acknowledge the undermining insults and name-calling that occur in their intimate relationships, the depth of the inner bruises, emotional pain, and eroded sense of self often remain hidden from conscious awareness. In many cases, somatic symptoms such as

1

headaches or stomach problems mask despair and profound loneliness.

Some writers have described emotional abuse as an adjunct of
physical abuse (Walker, 1984a). Tolman sees it as an integral part of
the humiliation inherent in physical battering. Because "physical
abuse has aspects of psychological maltreatment," he questions
whether it is possible to separate emotional and physical abuse: "In
addition to the physical pain and intimidation a woman may feel
when her husband slaps her in front of her child, she may also feel
humiliated, embarrassed, and demeaned. The latter feelings may
even be the more harmful and debilitating effects of this physically
abusive behavior" (Tolman, 1992, p. 293).

Emotional abuse may occur without physical abuse, however,
and its effects are just as powerful (J. B. Miller, personal communication, June 1993). Many women have described the devastating
effects of their partners' repeated put-downs and insulting labeling.
Being called *whore, bitch, crazy, stupid, unfaithful,* and *ugly* can
take a heavy toll on one's self-esteem, as Ginny affirms:

> How can I explain to people the terrible misery I feel when he laughs
> at my ideas and tells me I'm "silly" and have no understanding of oth-
> ers' motivations? I'm a good lawyer! I'm even being considered for a
> federal appointment. That's how my judgment is viewed in the com-
> munity. Yet he rolls his eyes and shakes his head in disgust, and I feel
> pain inside.

The most salient identifying characteristic of emotional abuse is
its patterned aspect. Couples in most relationships exchange isolated insults over time, but emotional abuse is not an occasional cutting remark made in the heat of argument. It is the clear and consistent pattern of these remarks, the ongoing effort to demean and
control, that constitutes emotional abuse. Tolman (1992) describes
a continuum ranging from "withdrawing momentarily, listening
unempathically, [and] speaking sharply in anger [to] . . . pervasive,
one-sided, severe psychological torture paralleling intentional
brainwashing and mistreatment of prisoners of war" (p. 292).

The pattern of emotional abuse occurs on two levels—overt and
covert—and utilizes several mechanisms of abuse. *Overt* abuse is
openly demeaning. Janie, a twenty-eight-year-old high school
teacher, described how her husband, Peter, a business manager, fre-

quently announced during family gatherings that she was incompetent and ineffective. He criticized her for burning toast, keeping a "dirty house," and being a "lousy sex partner." When they attended a social event together, he accused her of flirting with one of the guests and insisted she was having an affair. Although Peter described Janie as "ugly" and "fat," he was intensely jealous and convinced that other men were pursuing her. He carefully monitored her expenditures, discouraged her from attending social functions at school or with colleagues, and limited her visits to family members. He even restricted her telephone calls to her mother.

This overt pattern of isolation, jealousy, and/or control of finances is common in emotionally abusive relationships. Other overt forms include abusing the children in the presence of an adult victim, mistreating the victim's pets, and threatening violence toward her parents. The list of overt abusive behaviors (as shown in Exhibit 1) ranges from sulking and silence to verbal insults, control of schedule and activities, mild physical behavior (like slamming doors), and threatened and actual attacks against the spouse and others.

The second level of violence (Exhibit 2), *covert* emotional abuse, is more subtle but no less devastating to victims. Because they are often unaware of its essential violence, victims commonly react to covert abuse with feelings of despair and confusion.

This kind of abuse consists of an insidious, sometimes complex pattern of negative feedback. The film *Sleeping with the Enemy* (Goldberg & Rubin, 1991) provides a clear example of this sort of emotional abuse. In one scene, the victim has dressed for the evening, and her abusive partner disapproves of what she is wearing. His disgusted tone of voice as he cuts his eyes up and down her body, as well as his affect of resignation, send a clear covert message: She is totally inept at selecting her attire.

In a subsequent scene, she has changed to the dress he prefers, although its low back does not protect her from the evening chill (she had mentioned warmth as her reason for choosing the other dress). This is a typical abuser perspective. The *abuser's* comfort is the only organizing theme of his thoughts and actions. Any consistent empathy for the partner's feelings is precluded. By discounting her needs and feelings, he tells her, implicitly, how unimportant they are to him. Among emotional abuse victims, this constant and

---

OVERT MECHANISMS OF ABUSE

1. Belittling
2. Yelling
3. Name-calling
4. Criticizing
5. Ordering around
6. Sulking
7. Withholding affection
8. Ignoring
9. Isolating from family and friends
10. Monitoring time, activities
11. Attempting to restrict resources (finances, telephone)
12. Intefering with opportunities (job, medical care, education)
13. Accusing the victim of engaging in repeated, purposively hurtful behaviors
14. Throwing objects, not necessarily at the victim
15. Slamming of objects or doors
16. Ridiculing the victim
17. Expressing disgust toward the victim
18. Threatening to abandon (physically or emotionally)
19. Expressing excessive jealousy
20. Threatening life, pets, property, family
21. Exposing the victim to abuse of her children, pets, or parents
22. Coercing the victim into illegal activity
23. Provoking the victim into helpless flailing

Exhibit 1

subtle discounting of their feelings contributes to a profound sense of loneliness and sadness.

Different styles of covert abuse can convey the same message. Albert, a distinguished university professor, was well-known in the academic community for his research. He was frequently invited to colleges and professional meetings to give speeches and to present papers. Albert and his wife, Terry, had been married for seven years but had no children; he had decided, unilaterally, that the world was "not a fit place to raise children."

Through periodic expressions of exasperation, Albert clearly demonstrated that he found Terry's ideas unworthy of his consider-

---

COVERT MECHANISMS OF ABUSE

1. Discounting
2. Negation
3. Projection/accusation
4. Denial (of abuse by the abuser)
5. Negative labeling
6. Subtle threats of physical and/or emotional abandonment, or actual physical and or/emotional abandonment

---

Exhibit 2

ation. He sighed with disgust, shook his head in dramatic bewilderment, and used a patient yet strained tone of voice, as if he were talking to a slow child. Terry reacted with depression.

At times, his distaste for her feelings and ideas crossed the line between denigration and negation; he simply denied that they existed at all. In therapy, Terry described numerous incidents in which Albert commented, "You don't really feel that way," or "Terry, you do not think that." He frequently interrupted her during conversations and announced to friends that Terry thought or felt a particular way, although she had never expressed any such feeling or idea. She began to be confused about her real perceptions, wondering how she actually felt. During therapy Terry cried for long periods of time. She was unable to understand her feelings and was certain that she should not be crying. "My husband is so kind to me," she said repeatedly while describing her confusion and suicidal thoughts.

The impact of this depiction of one's feelings as unreal is powerful. The victim begins to internalize the negation and to feel herself eroding away. When Albert called her "stupid," "worthless," and "the brain-dead one," Terry felt as if she were "coming apart": "I come apart and lose touch with parts of myself—my ideas, values, and my style of behaving. I don't know myself anymore."

Over time these covert mechanisms of labeling, discounting, and negation lead to a diminution and destruction of the self. Victims describe feeling that the constituent parts of the self—the individual characteristics, abilities and skills, preferences and wishes, dreams and aspirations—no longer cohere. This fragmentation affects the victim's thinking and judgment. She may have uncontrollable intrusive thoughts and mental images that reinforce over and over the abuser's denigrating and negating labeling.

Terry had three automobile accidents (running a stop sign and two red lights) while she was mentally reviewing emotionally abusive exchanges she had with Albert. Although she sensed on one level that she was courting danger, she was unable to control her thoughts. The kinds of insistent ideas and mental images Terry experienced are characteristic of trauma. (The trauma of emotional abuse in particular is discussed in detail in Chapter 4.)

Terry and Albert's discussions often followed a familiar pattern. Albert would begin by calling Terry insulting names and by discounting and negating her feelings and ideas. She would begin to cry and feel desperate, trying to explain that she wished he would respect her ideas. Drawing himself up to an erect posture and puckering his lips, Albert would raise his eyebrows, shake his head, sigh like a martyr, and say in a hissing tone of voice, "Terry you are so sensitive—just like your mother said before we were married." Typically he added, "How difficult life is with an oversensitive individual like you." By projecting his own hypersensitivity onto Terry, Albert was denying his own contribution to the conflict.

There was a scriptlike quality to Albert's behavior during these exchanges. First he would begin to put on his coat, saying, "You cause deep problems for us, Terry." Then he would start toward the door in a covert threat of abandonment. Once when she asked if he would return, he answered, "Maybe yes, maybe no." If he did not, his attitude conveyed clearly, Terry was wholly to blame.

Albert counted on Terry's fear of abandonment. When he began putting on his coat, she would experience a panic attack and start hyperventilating. He would offer to stay if she would only behave "normally." She would apologize and cling to him; he would then take off his coat. Frightened that Albert would leave her, Terry would attempt to open conversations in which he refused to participate, and to hold hands with him or embrace him while he remained cold and aloof. Finally, sometime later in the evening, he would hug her back.

The powerful impact of a threat of abandonment (emotional and/or physical) is often unrecognized in the therapeutic community. An emotional abuse victim usually has a history of anxious attachment that makes her vulnerable to this type of threat. As a child, according to Bowlby (1973, 1988), the anxiously attached adult had parents who failed to hold her and provide a safe place in which to be anchored and connected; they did not provide a secure base of love and tenderness, nor did they listen to and understand their child's feelings and needs. In childhood many victims of emotional abuse did not receive the affectionate empathy described by Kohut (1986), nor did they experience nurturing figures who reflected back positively their developing selves. As a result, they lacked the important feeling of validation needed by growing children.

Instead, many of these children were brought up to fulfill the needs of adults (A. Miller, 1981), although the situation was seldom acknowledged by either parent or child. Often the child was expected to be a surrogate mother to her siblings or to take care of a physically or emotionally inadequate parent. Nurturing those who should be nurturing her, she grew up feeling unconnected, profoundly lonely, sad, and frightened.

Later in childhood—and in adulthood—this treatment can result in the kind of clinging behavior exhibited by Terry. Hoping to receive crumbs of warmth and connection, victims cling desperately (physically and emotionally) to nonnurturing figures like Albert. When they do not receive validation of themselves and are emotionally assaulted by those they live with on the most intimate terms, they feel betrayed.

With such a background and a relationship with an emotionally assaultive partner, a pattern of betrayals can lead to trauma. Overt and covert emotional abuse often generate a spiral of desperate clinging, subsequent betrayals, and more trauma. Judith Herman (1922, p. 56) describes how the terror of trauma intensifies the need for "protective attachments." The tragedy for emotional abuse victims is that the partner from whom they seek attachment is himself the source of betrayal and trauma. He is likely to respond with additional abuse and threats of abandonment.

When emotional abuse victims are abandoned, they experience a mourning process very similar to those of people grieving losses and beginning to heal from traumatic life events (Herman, 1992).

Repeatedly, emotional abuse victims describe feeling a dual loss: the loss of warmth and support from the partner and the loss of their sense of self.

There can be no comprehensive recognition of their problem, nor healing of the resultant trauma, without acknowledging and treating the anxious clinging. It reflects a deep and legitimate hunger for connection. Just as Herman stresses the need for reconnection of traumatized individuals with their communities, so too must traumatized emotional abuse victims reconnect both with their inner selves and with others. This is the journey toward becoming a survivor.

As mentioned earlier, people suffering from emotional abuse seldom recognize themselves as victims; for them, emotional violence has become a way of life. As the experience of being emotionally mistreated often begins early in childhood, the victim cannot conceive that another, entirely different kind of relationship is possible. Yet although they have become accustomed to emotional violence, they never cease to feel its pain. Each new wound is as devastating as the preceding demeaning assault.

Emotional abuse can also exist in the wider social context. In fact, the abuser's rules may resemble the kind of unfair rules enforced in families, institutions, and cultures based on inequality. As a result of these rules, individuals from one gender, religious, ethnic, or age group suffer various forms of overt or covert abuse that limit and define divisions of labor, social intercourse, and ownership of property or credit. Like individual victims of emotional abuse, these social victims may not envision a different way of life, or they may lack the skills needed to achieve institutional or social transformation.

Evelyn Nesby is an African-American individual who grew up in the Atlanta area during the 1930s. In her rural community, the female children and women gathered food, milked cows, picked berries, churned milk, and obeyed the male elders—even if it meant depriving the children of essentials. They were faced with the social inequality that forced the men to sell the property on which the family depended for its subsistence. "That was what we knew. We didn't know any other way to live" (E. Nesby, personal communication, June 1993).

The victim's sense that emotional violence is normal and inevitable is frequently reflected in her attempts to change the situation in ways that leave intact the abuser's right to denigrate her. Unable to imagine that the emotional violence could stop, she is likely to assume much of the blame for the troubled relationship and to attempt to improve it by changing her own behavior. Or she may try to extract some small crumb of validation from the resistant abuser.

The tragedy of the quest for loving responsiveness from an abuser is that it is doomed to result in profound loneliness and sadness. In extreme cases, the outcome is murder—of the victim by the abuser or the abuser by the victim. In 37 interviews with emotionally abused women charged with murdering their partners, I found two frequently mentioned themes: (1) fear of losing the partner, and (2) failed attempts to gain validation and affirmation just prior to the murder. Sometimes the abuser's threats to harm her have terrified the woman into striking out with a weapon.

Women who are both victims of abuse and perpetrators of illegal actions are sometimes referred for professional evaluation by attorneys. These *victim-perpetrators* have been convinced by emotional and/or physical abuse to obey their partner's orders, even when these orders involve check forging, murder, bombings, bank robberies, credit card theft, and drug dealing. When he is arrested, she is swept along in the web of intrigue and usually is charged as an accomplice.

Jan married Randy when she was only sixteen, and she spent ten years with him in spite of emotional and physical battering. During that time she had four miscarriages as a result of his beatings. Randy constantly labeled her "whore" and "worthless," and he isolated her from friends and family by moving from town to town. His racket involved stolen social security checks; Jan's role was to open bank accounts with the stolen checks and withdraw the money. When she tried to quit, Randy threatened to rape and hang their two small sons (who were two and five years old). Prior to each illegal transaction he would hold a gun to her head and say, "I wonder if I will shoot you today." Sometimes he would hold his fist in front of her face, threatening to hit her, as she and the two little boys cried and whimpered. Believing his threats, she continued to do his bidding until the FBI arrested them.

Other victim-perpetrators are coerced into unlawful behavior solely through emotional abuse. During her twelve-year relationship with Tony, Barb suffered a continuous stream of overt and covert emotional abuse. He sustained control over her through manipulation and threats of abandonment. She bought the ingredients Tony needed to make a bomb without realizing what he was doing. When he ordered her to take it to the post office and mail it, she complied.

During the psychosocial evaluation, Barb was confused and depressed. She described Tony's behavior: how he praised her and behaved affectionately while seeming to criticize and label her "stupid—without a good idea in your head" at the same time or shortly thereafter. Moments of holding her and kissing her tenderly alternated with expressions of deep rage. Barb grieved for the intermittent warmth and waited for its return. She never questioned his orders, nor how her assigned tasks fit into his goals.

> I never suspected he was building a bomb until I saw an article in the newspaper about the bombing. I had a fleeting thought that just maybe . . . then I said "no, that's just not possible." I did whatever he asked so he wouldn't get cold and go away from me in his head and heart. I wasn't allowed to go into the bathroom. He kept it padlocked, and only he had the key. Later I found out he'd built the bomb in there.

Isolated from her family and friends in another state, Barb clung to Tony for reassurance. He flew into a rage if a man so much as glanced at her. He selected her clothes and made all of the decisions, including when they would take a shower.

As these cases illustrate, the similarities between emotional abuse and the torture of prisoners are striking. Some prisoners are tortured to obtain information, but frequently their captors simply want to demean and intimidate people with differing political or ideological views. In *Revenge of the Apple*, Alicia Partnoy (1992) describes her experience as a prisoner in Argentina, where she was a "disappeared" human. That is, only the military authorities who kidnaped her knew her whereabouts. Her feelings and thoughts did not exist for her captors, who tortured prisoners indiscriminately and exercised total control over their lives and deaths.

Victims of emotional abuse, too, are isolated and experience a kind of disappearance (of the self). Like the prisoners, they are indiscriminately abused and lose control over their own destiny. Maria, a former political prisoner from a Latin American country, understood the similarities all too clearly. She described her relationship with her American lesbian lover as follows:

> This relationship is really every bit as painful as when I was in prison. She tells me I am silly, that my feelings aren't even there. She ignores me, ridicules my ideas, and scorns my views. And I feel the same scared and awful emptiness as when the prison guards beat me for expressing my views. I was captured then; I am captured now. One experience is no less powerful than the other. My headaches are just as painful in this relationship now as they were in prison. My self was taken then. It is taken now.

The diminution of the prisoner's self and the attempt to erase personal identities during incarceration is described by Viktor Frankl in *Man's Search for Meaning* (1963). The depersonalization of prisoners, a salient feature of the Nazi concentration camps, is also characteristic of emotional abuse. In the camps the prisoners' unique clothing and qualities were stripped away; all were required to dress and act alike. A similar attempt to wipe out the self's uniqueness occurs in emotional abuse.

Among the Holocaust victims and the "disappeared" of more recent history, the certainty of imminent death haunted prisoners. Among emotionally abused individuals who struggle to maintain a sense that their feelings and thoughts exist and are worthwhile, the threat of the disappearance of the self is similarly terrifying. They report feeling empty, confused, and terrorized when threatened with emotional assault and annihilation. "Panicked," "horrified," "scared," and "petrified" are characteristic descriptions of emotionally abused women facing the destruction of the sense of self.

Jennifer, the forty-eight-year-old wife of an emotionally abusive surgeon, faced something like an impending death:

> When he says my feelings and ideas are worthless, and I am a burden he finds disgusting, I feel like nothing inside. He says he wishes I were dead, and I feel dead inside. It is as if my self is dying and that there may be no coming back this time. I can't think or function well. I really feel like someone has come along and shot my insides, and there is only death and nothingness left. It's so scary. I am terrified.

Ginny, the lawyer, described a very similar feeling:

> My ideas and thoughts and feelings become fragmented until I believe I
> am drowning in an avalanche of his discounts and negations. Then—
> My God—I have disappeared, and I struggle. "Where are my pieces?" I
> cannot survive this much longer. I feel it would be better if I were hon-
> estly and totally dead instead of this dying inside and trying to come
> back together time after time.

Victims frequently suffer from physical problems—headaches,
stomachaches, and upper respiratory illness—that are metaphors
for the pain of emotional abuse. Ginny, who had frequent attacks
of bronchitis and asthma, realized in therapy that "I often lost my
voice when I got bronchitis, but it made no difference, since nothing I said counted in the relationship anyway. Though my head and
stomach ached, it was really my heart that was aching. There was
no space for me to be myself, so I couldn't breathe."

Because its symptoms are so varied and so well disguised, emotional abuse is difficult to recognize. The intrusive thoughts and
flashbacks often experienced by emotional abuse victims (Chapter
4) are frequently mistaken for psychotic hallucinations, obsessive-
compulsive ideation, or simply resistance to change.

Moreover, the scarcity of a diagnostic perspective that specifically recognizes the repeated nature of the trauma makes it particularly difficult to diagnose emotional abuse. Herman (1992) suggests
that the absence of this perspective regarding chronicity causes
therapists to make diagnostic errors when working with other individuals who experience ongoing trauma:

> The persistent anxiety, phobias, and panic of survivors are not the
> same as ordinary anxiety disorders. The somatic symptoms of survivors
> are not the same as ordinary psychosomatic disorders. Their depression
> is not the same as ordinary depression. And the degradation of their
> identity and relational life is not the same as ordinary personality disor-
> der. (p. 118)

She points out that the lack of a clear perspective of traumatization
by ongoing stress means that mental health professionals may not
recognize "the connection between the patient's present symptoms
and the traumatic experience" (p. 118).

Making that connection is the first essential step toward helping these victims. Therapists and advocates can treat emotional abuse—once they recognize it as the powerful form of violence it is. In Chapter 2, therefore, I discuss in detail the differentiation of emotional abuse from other forms of abuse.

Its victims' cries for help are not, alas, always clear, for they are often unaware of the source of their suffering. But their invisible wounds can result in desperation, confusion, accidents, and even suicide.

They say
I speak too softly,
that I am practically mumbling,
that they can't hear
the screams piercing. (Partnoy, 1992, p. 97).

2

Differentiating Emotional Abuse

Marti Tamm Loring & David L. Myers

M artin (1976) and Walker (1984a, 1984b) view the emotional abuse of women as one aspect of their physical abuse by men. Other researchers have variously characterized emotional abuse as *nonphysical abuse* (Hudson & McIntosh, 1981), *indirect abuse* (Gondolf, 1985), *emotional abuse* (NiCarthy, 1986), *psychological abuse* (Patrick-Hoffman, 1982; Walker, 1984b), *psychological aggression* (Murphy & O'Leary, 1989), *psychological maltreatment* (Tolman, 1989), and *mental* or *psychological torture* (Russell, 1982).

Regardless of the terminology, this type of violence—fraught with degradation, fear, and humiliation—has been described by Fortune (1991) as the most painful and by Ferraro (1979) as the most detrimental to self-esteem. It dismembers the victim's self by systematically attacking her personality, style of communication, accomplishments, values, and dreams. This violence can bring on profound depression and illness, automobile accidents, suicide, and murder of the abuser.

To help its victims, therapists and advocates must first be able to identify this destructive process. The challenge of differentiating emotional abuse from other forms of violence, especially physical abuse, must always precede effective intervention. To make an accurate diagnosis, mental health professionals and other intervention specialists will need to focus on several factors, including the specific mechanisms of abuse employed, the nature of abuser-abused relationships, and the timing of abuse.

15

Various researchers have studied the mechanisms of emotional abuse described in Chapter 1, principally in the context of physical battering. The most obvious forms of overt verbal abuse—insults, name-calling, and threats of violence or abandonment—have received the most attention in the psychological literature.[1] Tolman has also studied such subtle forms of verbal abuse as discounting the woman's ideas or feelings and blaming her for the man's own problems or for his recourse to violence: Other forms of emotional abuse studied include jealousy, possessiveness, and isolating the victim from friends and family.[2]

Related work by Marshall (1992) has explored what she terms "symbolic violence"—such intimidating behaviors as kicking a wall, smashing furniture or dishes, driving recklessly with the victim in the car, and throwing objects about. Even milder forms of violence (shaking a finger at the victim, making threatening gestures or faces, or shaking his fist) carry symbolic threats of violence. Other such behaviors studied by Marshall include destroying or threatening to damage objects the victim cares about, and "acting like he wants to kill her" (p. 114).

A characteristic kind of attachment binds victim and abuser. It is not an empathic connection between two separate, equal individuals. Rather, the abuser perceives the victim in terms of his own needs and wishes, while the victim struggles to connect with him in a mutually validating and empathic manner. When her efforts are repeatedly met with scornful refusals and other forms of emotional abuse, the victim becomes traumatized and clings ever more desperately to the abuser.

Bowlby's work on anxious attachment explains the antecedents of this clinging behavior. As noted in Chapter 1, he has shown that children experience fears of abandonment as a result of emotional deprivation—the absence of physical or emotional warmth and empathy from significant adults. Later in life, when the abusive adult

---

1. See, for example, Follingstad, Rutledge, Berg, Hause, and Polek (1990), Borkowski, Murch, and Walker (1983), Ewing (1987), Follingstad and Neckerman (1988), Hofeller (1982), Murphy and O'Leary (1989), Steinmetz (1977), Straus (1974), and Straus, Gelles, and Steinmetz (1988).

2. See Hilberman and Munson (1977–1978), Hofeller (1982), Rounsaville (1978), Douglas (1987), Ewing (1987), Walker (1983, 1984), and Tolman (1989).

partner criticizes and/or withdraws from the victim, the same fears are triggered and result in desperate clinging behavior.

Another important issue, related to the timing of abuse, has been raised by two studies of physically battered women. First, Murphy and O'Leary (1989) report finding a progressive abuse process: although only psychological aggression may be present early in the relationship, it tends to escalate into physical aggression within the first thirty months of marriage. Second, Walker (1984a, 1984b) has identified a cycle of violence—gradually increasing tension leading to an explosion of violence (primarily physical battering), followed by a "honeymoon period" free of abuse and characterized by contrition on the part of the abuser.

Are women who are emotionally abused but not physically battered subject to a similar cycle of violence? Do they experience periods that are free of abuse, or is emotional abuse more continuous? Because it has been considered principally an adjunct of physical abuse, emotional abuse has not been studied as a separate phenomenon. In contrast, our research has compared the two types of abuse along several dimensions (Loring & Myers, 1991). These dimensions emerged through lengthy interviews with 121 emotionally abused, physically battered, and nonabused women. Because the physically abused women also reported emotional abuse in their relationships, the study actually differentiated between women who were emotionally and physically abused and those who were emotionally but not physically abused.

The subjects were married women (aged nineteen to seventy-eight years old) living in the Atlanta area. They were referred by professionals in law, human services, medicine, law enforcement, mental health, and social services to the Center for Mental Health and Human Development. They ranged in socioeconomic status from low to high. For comparison purposes, the study also included a group of women who had experienced neither emotional nor physical abuse in their current relationships. The study was based on an average of nine hours of clinical interviews over 6 sessions with each woman and on two unstructured interviews (each approximately three hours long) with both the woman and her husband.

The specific hypotheses of the study were, first, that women who experienced emotional abuse but not physical battering could be readily located, and second, that physically battered and emotionally abused groups of women would differ in two respects: (1) in the pattern of abuse, with emotionally abused women experiencing an ongoing, linear pattern of abuse, compared with the alternating cycle of violence reported for physically battered women; and (2) in the victim's awareness of being abused, with emotionally abused women less likely than physically abused women to think of themselves as victims of violence. During a loosely structured interview, researchers asked each woman a series of questions and invited her to discuss a wide range of relevant topics. (See Exhibit 3 for the list of questions asked during the interview.) The women in both abused groups cried frequently during the interviews and often related lengthy anecdotes and examples of abuse.

The behavior observed during interviews with the couples provided evidence bearing on a number of the interview questions. For example, every male partner of the emotionally abused and physically battered women raised his voice at some point in the interviews. Most of these men interrupted the women and were both condescending and sarcastic. Many referred to the woman or her behavior as "stupid," "silly," or "dumb." Because some of the men were unwilling to come to the center, several interviews were conducted in the couple's home. Many of the women and men in the study were subsequently referred for therapy.

Analysis of the data identified seven variables that differentiated the three groups of women:

1. Self-reporting of emotional abuse
2. History of emotional abuse in the woman's family of origin
3. Presence of anxious attachment: frequent and patterned emotions and behavior indicating the woman's fear of abandonment, and her verbal, emotional, and physical clinging to her husband
4. Covert communication abuse: the husband's physical or emotional withdrawal, subtle discounts and negation of her statements and feelings, negative labeling, and projection of blame and his own feelings onto the woman
5. Linear verbal abuse: continuous, noncyclic overt and covert abuse (yelling, name-calling, criticism, emotional withdrawal, subtle discounts and negations, projection of blame or feelings onto the victim)

INTERVIEW QUESTIONS ASKED OF ALL WOMEN

1. How many years have you been in your present marriage?

2. How many times have you been hit (with fist, hand, or other object) in your present marriage?

3. How many times have your been shoved in your present marriage?

4. How many times have you been held down in your present marriage?

5. What was the year in which your answer to question number 2 first occured, if applicable?

6. What was the first year in which your answer to question number 3 first occured, if applicable?

7. What was the first year in which your answer to question number 4 first occured, if applicable?

8. Was hitting, etc., a reoccurring event or did it occur one, two, three, or how many times? What year in the marriage did it first occur?

9. Do you consider yourself emotionally abused? If so, why; what happens?

10. Were you physically or emotionally abused as a child?

11. In question number 10 (if applicable), by whom?

12. Did your mother yell at you?

13. Did your father yell at you?

14. Did your mother call you names?

15. Did your father call you names?

16. Were your ideas and feelings respected by parents?

17. Did your mother and/or father (which) make fun of you?

18. Were your feelings ignored or treated as unworthy?

19. Did you feel valued?

20. Does your husband yell at you?

21. Does your husband call you names?

22. Does your husband respect your ideas and feelings?

23. Does your husband make fun of you?

24. Are your feelings ignored or treated as unworthy by your husband?

25. Do you feel valued by your husband; do you feel your ideas are negated or discounted?

26. Are you often blamed for things, labeled in some way, when this is a reflection of his hurt, anger, anxiety, etc.?

27. Describe your attachment to your husband: Are you someone who clings? (look for patterns of clinging and fear of abandonment)

28. Are you physically abused in any way in your current relationship?

29. If you or your referring therapist or friend think you are emotionally abused, does it happen once in a while or often with breaks? Or is it continuous and ongoing without breaks?

30. Do you feel lonely and/or confused during communication with your husband? (get frequency and severity)

Exhibit 3

6. Reporting of loneliness and confusion
7. Presence (or absence) of physical abuse

All the variables except the first were based on information drawn from the two interviewers' clinical judgment of the woman's self-reporting, observation of the couple's interaction and the husband's behavior, and responses to the interview questions and other topics. The assignment of information to the seven variables was reviewed and corroborated independently by a third therapist. In conducting this review, the third rater was unaware of both the experimental hypotheses and the group to which the original interviewers had assigned each woman.

Out of hundreds of judgments, the third therapist disagreed with the original two interviewers in only three instances, which were resolved through discussion. A chi-square test was used to evaluate the significance of the differences between the emotionally abused women and the other two groups. Table 1 summarizes the data for all three groups.

The interview with the emotionally abused group provided numerous examples of covert communication abuse—discounts, negation, projection, denial, negative labeling, and abandonment. Each woman in this group reported that her husband habitually implied that her feelings and ideas were inadequate and insignificant. This insidious violence clearly had a powerful negative effect on these women's lives. Its subtle destructiveness was harder to bear than overt threats and criticisms.

> My husband sometimes calls me stupid. At other times he conveys his attitude toward my ideas and feelings by simply ignoring me when I talk, sighing loudly when I discuss my dreams for the future, and laughing while shaking his head in disgust when I describe an idea.

These women reported being ignored when they spoke and being advised frequently "You don't know what you're talking about: Consult someone who knows about that." Typical undermining comments were "That doesn't make sense" and "How can you feel that way?" Although the physically abused women also described instances of covert communication abuse, they focused principally on fears of physical harm or death.

In spite of her husband's scorn for her ideas, every emotionally

TABLE 1. Emotionally Abused, Nonabused, and Physically Abused Women.

					Variables			
Group	No.	Emotional abuse in present marriage	Emotional abuse in family of origin	Clinging and fear of abandonment	Covert communication abuse by husband	Overt and covert communication abuse by husband	Feelings of loneliness and confusion	One or more incidents of physical abuse by husband
Emotionally abused women	28	29%	100%	100%	100%	100%	100%	0%
Physically abused women	40	68%*	65%*	80%*	73%*	0%*	85%*	100%*
Nonabused women	34	0%	0%	6%	6%*	3%*	3%*	0%

* Significant difference with emotionally abused women, $p < .05$.

abused woman in the study longed for his "affirmation," "respect," and "belief in me." Most reported a yearning to "feel good about myself" in the current marriage relationship, but far more often than the women in either of the other groups, they expressed profound loneliness and sadness. They described their feelings as "desperate" and "unconnected":

> All my life I felt that the people close to me did not listen or hear what I said. So I felt alone in the world and lonely. I still do—unconnected and deeply lonely.

Invariably such women were fearful that their husbands would leave them, either emotionally or physically. They spoke of this anxiety with greater intensity and frequency than women in the other two groups. Many of the emotionally abused women cried, used words like *"terrified,"* and disclosed that they lived in constant fear of abandonment.

There were substantial differences among the three groups on the issue of self-reporting of abuse. While more than half the women in the physically abused group responded that they considered themselves emotionally abused (question 9), less than a third of the emotionally abused women viewed themselves in this way. Nonetheless, the latter unanimously reported covert communication abuse by their husbands, feelings of loneliness and confusion, and behavior interpreted as indicative of anxious attachment. Approximately 70 percent of the physically abused women reported these experiences.

The women in both categories of abuse were subject to high levels of overt and covert emotional abuse. Most either reported or were observed during the couples interviews to experience overt forms of emotional abuse—being yelled at, called names, or ridiculed. All twenty-eight women categorized as emotionally abused, and 72 percent (twenty-nine out of forty) of the physically abused, experienced covert communication abuse during the interviews. No such pattern of covert abuse was uncovered for the nonabused women.

On all seven variables, emotionally abused women differed substantially from the other two groups. A major difference was in the crucial issue of the timing of abuse. All of the emotionally abused—but none of the physically abused women—reported a linear and virtually continuous pattern of overt and covert verbal abuse. This contrasts with the cyclic pattern Walker (1984b) found with physical abuse. Moreover, significantly more of the emotionally abused group than the other 2 groups reported the presence of other variables: 100% of the emotionally abused women, and 65 to 85 percent of the physically abused women, but few of the nonabused women reported a history of emotional abuse, current anxious attachment, or loneliness and confusion.

Emotionally abused women also differed in their tendency to be unaware of the abuse. Only eight of the twenty-eight (29 percent) emotionally abused women saw themselves as abused, whereas twenty-seven of the forty (67 percent) physically abused women recognized that their relationship involved emotional as well as physical abuse.

All the emotionally abused women, and 65 percent of the physically abused women, but none of the nonabused women reported a history of emotional abuse in their families of origin. In fact, few of the nonabused women reported the presence of any of the seven factors. It seems probable, therefore, that a childhood free from emotional abuse increases the likelihood that a woman will not marry, or stay with, an emotionally abusive partner.

This study establishes clearly that a distinct group of women exists who are emotionally but not physically abused. The average length of the marriages (11.2 years) suggests that emotional abuse is not necessarily a transient stage leading to physical abuse, as argued by Murphy and O'Leary (1989). Nonetheless, among the women most heavily studied to date, emotional abuse is in fact a precursor of or occurring-jointly with physical battering. In the heretofore unrecognized group of emotional abuse victims uncovered by the present study, physical abuse did not occur.

The study also supports other work (Follingstad et al., 1990; Walker, 1984b) suggesting that emotional abuse is just as devastating as physical abuse. When the powerful impact of emotionally violent behavior is better understood, the added pain of physical battering will not be viewed as necessary to legitimize emotional violence. Therapists and advocates will learn to recognize the insidiousness of emotional abuse even when it does not lead to physical violence.

The Atlanta study derives its data from the experience of emotionally abused, physically abused, and nonabused women from a limited sample of married women. Clearly, more research is needed. Subsequent studies should explore emotional abuse in other contexts: women in dating and cohabitating relationships, men emotionally abused by women, and same-sex emotional violence in lesbian and gay relationships. The present study may also underestimate the extent of emotional abuse in the subjects' families of origin. Some women in the study may have experienced emotional abuse in childhood without being aware of it and so were unable to report it.

Further studies of the powerful impact of covert abuse on the victim are badly needed. Too many women have described the anguish and desperation they have suffered from this form of violence. In some cases, the emotional violence has triggered suicide attempts or murder of the abuser. Even when the results are less obviously dire, the tragedy of despair and loss of the human connection can and does occur. In Chapter 3, I explore that loss of connection and the futile attempts of emotionally abused women to achieve attachment with the abuser.

3

Attachment

Disruption of connection is the core of emotional abuse, while the struggle to attach is the hallmark of the emotionally abused woman. The typical abuser moves in and out of bonding with the victim, periodically sharing warmth and empathy, then cutting them off with overt and covert abuse. Confused by the intermittent connection and struggling to regain it, the victim clings anxiously to the abuser. Her harsh self-blame echoes the abuser's demeaning comments and becomes an internalized shaming mechanism, diminishing self-esteem and eroding the sense of self. Although she is usually not explicitly aware of the disconnection, the victim feels unaccountably sad, isolated, and profoundly lonely.

Attachment, which denotes one individual's struggle to bond with another, is not necessarily a mutual process. A victim of emotional abuse usually continues to seek attachment with an abuser who has withdrawn his affection. Hoping to regain the lost warmth, she may cling to him tenaciously. Attachment, in this specialized sense, is therefore different from *connection*, a relationship characterized by each partner's efforts to empathize with and respond to the other.

People who are connected recognize and respect differences between themselves. Consciously or intuitively, they realize that bonding styles are highly individual. One person's approach to a close personal relationship may involve frequent exchanges of views, earnest discussions about problems, and open displays of affection and expressions of anger. A more reserved person may feel comfortable having fewer conversations and problem-solving sessions, expressing affection privately, and avoiding angry confrontations. When couples attempt to accommodate to each other's style of attachment, the more verbal partner will make a conscious effort to cut back on problem-solving discussions, while the less verbal person will strive to open up more often.

In emotional abuse, there is no such respect or attempt to compromise. Instead the abuser ridicules and demeans the victim's style of attachment and other unique forms of relating. His behavioral repertoire is limited and is driven by his fear of loss and need to control. He displays little care and consideration for his partner or her feelings, and he ignores one of the essential components of the caring process—increasing knowledge and understanding of the other person in order to find better ways of responding to him or her (Mayeroff, 1971).

As noted in the preceding chapters, vulnerability to emotional abuse generally has its origins in childhood experiences. Babies and children who experience consistent empathy, understanding, and validation from a nurturing figure develop a sense of security and a comfortable pattern of attachment. The safe haven provided by certainty that the nurturer will be there in a kindly and warm manner most of the time endows the child with feelings of trust and hope for the future. When the nurturer mirrors back positively the child's responses to her environment, the seeds of her sense of self are planted and nourished. She feels unique and confident, excited about her own abilities and skills. Attachment to the nurturing parent provides a secure base from which to venture forth and explore the world (Bowlby, 1988).

Securely attached children hold onto nurturers tightly and are, in turn, consistently embraced with firmness and warmth. Even when the nurturer is occasionally unavailable or sad, the certainty of physical and emotional reunification (consistently established over time) remains, and no harm is done. The child is not panicked or traumatized by such infrequent physical and/or emotional absences. Generally this ebb and flow of secure attachment is carried over into adult relationships. Partners who establish the trust and certainty of being there for each other during difficult times fulfill their individual needs as well.

Infants and children who lack this secure and empathic foundation may become "anxiously attached" (Bowlby, 1973, 1979, 1988). This pattern is sometimes established when illness or depression limits a parent's physical or emotional accessibility to the child, or divorce or separation consume a parent's emotional resources for a long period. Similarly, the prolonged hospitalization or death of one parent often disrupts the development of normal attachment; the child may grow up emotionally abandoned. In childhood and in later life, this sense of abandonment can result in the desperate clinging described in some of the cases cited in Chapter 1.

Bowlby's studies of children physically or emotionally separated from their parents for considerable periods of time reveal this pattern of "anxious attachment" and strong clinging behavior under the following conditions (Bowlby, 1979, p. 137):

- When one or both parents either consistently fail to respond to or actively reject the child's efforts to elicit parental care
- During discontinuities of parenting occurring more or less frequently (for example, periods of hospitalization or divorce in which the nurturing figure is emotionally and/or physical absent)
- When a parent persistently threatens to withdraw his or her love as a means of discipline
- When one parent threatens to abandon the family, either to punish the child or to coerce the adult partner
- When one parent threatens to desert or kill the other parent or to commit suicide
- When guilt is induced by telling the child that his or her behavior will cause a parent's illness or death

Bowlby (1973) found that a child blamed for a parent's depression will blame herself and become prey to anxiety and fears of abandonment. She will cling all the more desperately to the parent or, in his or her absence, to reassuring fantasies of closeness. If an emotionally distant parent persists in pushing the child away and punishing her, a vicious circle is likely to ensue: the child reaches out for affection and validation again and again, and the nurturer pushes her away in each instance. Each time the cycle is repeated, the child feels more anxious and clings more desperately.

Joanie is a five-year-old whose mother, Susan, experienced sexual abuse as a child. Susan still suffers periodic bouts of depression. During what the family calls "one of her spells," she shuts herself in her room and cries until her husband returns from work. Meanwhile, Joanie's eleven-year-old brother fixes his sister's lunch and takes care of her. When her mother emerges, Joannie rushes to her and hangs on her skirts, sometimes jerking on them to gain attention. The attention, when it comes, is harsh: Susan screams at the child, "Leave me alone!" But Joannie clings all the more tightly. She also bids for her mother's attention by trying to engage her in conversation, demanding to be fed frequently, and complaining of frequent stomachaches and headaches.

For children like Joanie, repeated experiences of emotional abandonment induce deep yearnings and unfulfilled hopes for more consistent closeness. The child develops ambivalent emotions: a desperate hope for intimacy, and a despairing suspicion that she will never attain it. Moreover, she has experienced a repetitive cycle of reaching out and being rejected that can set the pattern of her adult life.

The emotionally abused child—and, later, the same child as an emotionally abused adult—treasures the precious nuggets of warmth and understanding she receives from the abuser. They are her lifeline and the basis of her sense of worth. She holds tenaciously to these occasional moments of empathic connection. When they are withdrawn, she mourns their loss and tries desperately to regain them. Recapturing them and transforming them into a more consistent, empathic, and lasting connection becomes her major quest in life.

An emotional abuse victim may even engage in a simultaneous quest for genuine connection with both the emotionally abusive parent and her own emotionally abusive partner. The grief and the struggle to regain the lost warmth and affirmation of both distant and more recent pasts is intense, as Bowlby (1979) describes it:

> With his whole emotional being, it seems, a bereaved person is fighting fate, trying desperately to turn back the wheel of time and to recapture the happier days that have been suddenly taken from him. So far from facing reality and trying to come to terms with it, a bereaved person is locked in a struggle with the past. (p. 95)

Thus the emotionally abused adult is caught in a dilemma. By choosing for her life partner a person as incapable of consistent empathic bonding as her parent, she is attempting to reconstruct a lost childhood. Although victims often report tantalizing moments in which the abuser seems to connect with genuine empathy and encouragement, such moments do not last. The longed-for bond with a consistently warm and responsive partner is simply not available in an emotionally abusive relationship. Yet the quest goes on. As one victim explains, it is "a struggle to collect crumbs of warmth and not let them get away."

Most couples, of course, experience periods of conflict and times when one partner's preoccupations separate him or her from the other. The harsh, unrelenting assaults and withdrawal in an emotionally abusive relationship are very different. They often have a scriptlike pattern, noted earlier, that is well illustrated by the experiences of Elizabeth, a forty-one-year-old former debutante who dropped out of college at nineteen and married to please her mother. At the time she began therapy Elizabeth had two children, a ten-year-old son and a six-year-old daughter. She was suffering from headaches for which no medical basis could be found.

> My mother was never warm or encouraging, just demanding. She preferred my two older brothers to me. I think that she was depressed and bored with being a housewife, so I was supposed to be all that she never was. She never hugged me or said she loved me and always seemed preoccupied with something else. I didn't feel listened to, never thought she ever really knew who I was or what interested me—which was drawing and painting. I've had headaches ever since I was a child, as if I was aching for warmth and affection.

When she married a socially prominent man ten years older than she was, Elizabeth hoped he would provide the missing attention and affection,

> unlike my father, who never spoke up or protected me when my mother called me "plain" and "ugly." But my husband was just like my mother, ordering me around and telling me what to wear. He never really protected me. Sometimes he was understanding though, and I kept trying to get him to stay that way, but the warmth always disappeared. I missed it so much! I wanted so badly to keep that feeling of

being connected with him, and I thought it was my fault when it went away.

Elizabeth felt sad and lonely when her husband withdrew emotionally. She became even lonelier when he began his emotional assaults and abrupt disconnections:

> I felt like I'd lost a friend. When he'd get mad and call me names, he said he'd like to drive the "right way to do things into my stupid head." He was pounding on me with his words. I felt so alone.

The emotional abuse was constant and unrelenting, although she did not recognize it as abuse until she began therapy. Elizabeth's husband criticized her clothes and her friends, and he isolated her from family and friends. When she started working in a store, he suspected her of having affairs with coworkers. But the subtle abuse was the most painful and wore away her sense of security and trust. How could she be open with her ideas and feelings when they were consistently ridiculed and misperceived?

> I just couldn't understand what had happened during a discussion full of his accusations. I would go over it in my mind over and over. He'd say, "Oh, no, dear, we don't feel that way at all." Or, "Are you imagining things again?" Or, "My dear, that is just too silly to discuss." And I would begin to feel depressed and try to explain how I really felt. Then he would pull away emotionally, looking at me coolly and starting to read a book without answering my questions. I kept trying, but I began to lose a sense of trust that he would be there for me, and that was scary.

Using withdrawal as a mechanism of control is emotional abandonment. The victim feels betrayed and isolated by the unilateral disconnection. As her need for connection grows, her attempts to engage the partner increase in frequency and intensity, and she clings harder. Although her efforts fail, the trauma of pain and terror leave the victim with no choice but to continue trying. Miller (1988) argues that

> the most terrifying and destructive feeling that a person can experience is isolation. . . . It is feeling locked out of the possibility of human connection. This feeling of desperate loneliness is usually accompanied by the feeling that you, yourself, are the reason for the exclusion. . . . And

you feel helpless, powerless, unable to act to change the situation. People will do almost anything to escape this combination of condemned isolation and powerlessness. (p. 5)

The attachment is so essential to her that the victim may obey the abuser's orders to commit illegal acts; to disobey him is to risk abandonment or emotional assault. Threats of abandonment create fear, uncertainty, and confusion for a victim whose sense of self is destroyed and who cannot therefore think through a problem effectively, nor comfort herself in moments of sadness. In this type of emotional abuse the victim's judgment is confused, and the abuser uses coercion to control her feelings of safety and well-being.

Margaret, a sixty-two-year-old African-American woman, experienced emotional abuse and attachment struggles throughout her marriage. At times she has also suffered physical abuse, which she found less painful. She felt that she had lost her sense of self amidst her husband's constant criticisms and threats. When pressured to forge signatures on unemployment checks for fake employees of his business, she complied, fearing that he would abandon her if she refused.

> Bruce, my husband, pushed me down several times during our forty-three years of marriage. But mostly it was his criticisms, over and over—of my cooking, appearance, way of talking, choice of clothes, ideas about anything—that hurt me so much. Sometimes he gave me flowers and was warm to me, but most of the time he put me down, saying I was fat and stupid. I was most frightened when he threatened to leave me, and I'd do anything to please him and keep him nice to me.

At first Margaret resisted when Bruce ordered her to forge signatures on the checks, but she relented after he refused to talk to her or hold her for a week. When the police arrested him for check fraud, Margaret was charged as an accomplice. At that time her lawyer obtained a judge's order for a psychosocial evaluation, and I agreed to make the assessment.

The assessment is called "psychosocial" because it incorporates components of the victim's relational and community connections as well as her psychological condition. The evaluation indicated that Margaret was a victim-perpetrator, an emotionally abused individual who obeyed her abuser in response to threats of emotional violence and (especially) abandonment. Like that of many other victims, Margaret's anxious attachment was tied to her past. She remembered her father's threats to leave the family and her own childhood fears that he would abandon her. Bruce's threats to leave her were a similarly powerful tool of coercion.

There are several reasons why, like Margaret, the typical victim does not view leaving an emotionally abusive relationship as an option. Usually she is unaware that what is occurring is emotional abuse. Even if she complains about her partner's verbal attacks, she usually lacks a full understanding of their impact on her. Furthermore, her complaints are often weakened by the abuser's denial and projection of blame. Desperate and despairing, she is likely to blame herself for the conflicts in the relationship.

Furthermore, the pervasive erosion of the self wrought by the abuse has left her unable to break out of the relationship. Her self-esteem is so diminished that the abuse is an echo of her own self-criticisms. Thoughts of severing her already diminished self from what she perceives as its only anchor are likely to precipitate panic attacks. Moreover, many victims of emotional abuse have never experienced a kinder and more consistently warm relationship and so cannot see any alternative to the present situation.

If a victim does decide to separate from the abuser, it is generally because of her attachment to and concern for her children. Carrie is a thirty-year-old businesswoman who successfully operates her own business. She became concerned about the impact of emotional abuse on her children:

> I never seriously considered separating from my husband during our twelve-year marriage. I think the thing that pushed me over the edge was finally realizing that my kids were being hurt by his treatment of me. I couldn't have left for myself because, as I later discovered, there wasn't enough self to leave for. He said I never did anything right. He acted like he despised me. Like I was dirt on the floor. He talked to me in a disgusted tone of voice, saying things like, "I just hate you so much." I started seeing my little boy treating my little girl like that, and I realized I had to do something.

During therapy Carrie related how relieved she felt when she was divorced and the abuse ceased. She regained the sense of self the emotional abuse process had destroyed.

I wouldn't go back for anything. I couldn't. I'd die before I'd stay with him one more day. And I mean it, I would die inside. I would go back to quitting living and stop being myself. I couldn't grow; I couldn't be a person with him. He wouldn't let me. He wanted me to be whatever he set his mind on. I feel so relieved now. It's so different. I feel like me again.

Prior to the separation Carrie experienced multiple somatic complaints. Although she later saw these physical symptoms as metaphors for her troubled attachment to her husband, at the time she did not understand their meaning or consider leaving the painful relationship:

> Looking back, I realize I was turning the emotional abuse into physical symptoms. I couldn't eat much and lost twenty-five pounds in one year. I had migraines and stomachaches the doctor could find no medical reason for. I think I had all these things wrong with me because of the power of the emotional abuse. The aches I thought were inside me were coming from the abuse outside. It made me ache with pain. I also had bronchitis, and sometimes I would lose my voice. I think that was a metaphor for losing my voice in the relationship. It was a terrible kind of attachment that had hold of me.

The emotionally abusive bonding left Carrie feeling so defeated and despairing that she was plagued with thoughts and images of suicide:

> If it hadn't been for my two children, I would have killed myself one night. I sat in the car all night long, thinking I was going to turn on the ignition and die from breathing carbon monoxide. But I knew my children would have to grow up with the knowledge that their mother had killed herself. I couldn't do that to them. But that's the only thing that kept me from doing it. What a terrible kind of attachment!

In therapy, victims like Carrie often seek help with their somatic symptoms or to deal with depression. In initial interviews they are unlikely to mention their troubled relationship, frequent accidents, or the deep despair that is all too evident in their demeanor. Little by little the therapist's questions elicit information about their hopelessness, self-blame, intense loneliness, and interactions with partners.

With help, victims of emotional abuse can begin to recognize the violence of the "terrible kind of attachment" that permeates their lives. They can learn that the abusive mechanisms diminishing their sense of self are not the necessary cost of a human connection. They can begin to envision new and different ways of bonding. As their quest for warmth and validation in one-sided attachments becomes a search for a mutually empathic connection—a place where she will be appreciated and allowed to flourish—the victim can move toward becoming a survivor.

At present, however, the trauma that results from this sort of abusive attachment is not well understood in the therapeutic community. In Chapter 4, therefore, I examine in some detail the relationship between trauma and emotional abuse, especially as it relates to the destruction of the self.

4

The Trauma of Emotional Abuse

In recent years the therapeutic literature has extensively explored the mechanisms and effects of trauma in such areas of human violence as wartime atrocities and child abuse. To date, however, the profession has not focused on the relationship between trauma and emotional abuse. Nor has it recognized that emotional abuse occurring without physical battering has its own unique process of traumatic development. Nonetheless, the suffering inflicted on victims of emotional abuse is as intense and pervasive as that experienced by other trauma victims; it can lead to a diminished or annihilated sense of self and to the terror that is characteristic of Post-Traumatic Stress Disorder (PTSD; American Psychiatric Association [APA], 1987).

In fact, many symptoms of emotional abuse—nightmares, intrusive thoughts, flashbacks, difficulty sleeping and concentrating, and psychogenic amnesia (APA, 1987)—are characteristic of PTSD. In this chapter I will discuss the relationship of emotional abuse to other kinds of trauma and describe several traumatic symptoms that are specific to this form of abuse.

Comparing Emotional Abuse to Other Forms of Trauma

During PTSD an individual experiences shocking, horrible, and unthinkable events that have a powerful impact on the mind and emotions (APA, 1987). Trauma can result from both natural disasters, like tornadoes and earthquakes, and from human violence. Trauma is a normal reaction to severe shock. An event like rape is shocking because it is unexpected and extremely painful. The victim often feels stunned, bewildered, betrayed; it is difficult to believe it is really happening. Subsequently, she may refuse to believe in the reality of the assault. In cases of childhood incest, victims may so completely repress knowledge of the abuse that they remain unaware of it for years—even while experiencing its traumatic effects.

Victims of emotional assault from a life companion experience a similar sense of shock and disbelief after each incident of abuse. What could be more unthinkable, more shocking than cruelty and degradation in what is supposed to be a loving, caring, nurturing partnership? The accurate term for marital abuse—"intimate violence" (Marshall, 1992, p. 105)—seems contradictory. Isn't the essence of intimacy gentleness and nonviolence? Like children who live through incest, many adult victims of emotional abuse report feeling shocked and betrayed. The abuser's emotional attacks are experienced as symbolic equivalents of a rape of the self.

DSM-III-R (APA, 1987) defines PTSD as the result of an event that is

> outside the range of usual human experience. . . . The stressor producing this syndrome would be markedly distressing to almost anyone, and is usually experienced with intense fear, terror, and helplessness. The characteristic symptoms involve reexperiencing the traumatic event. . . . The disorder is apparently more severe and longer lasting when the stressor is of human design. (pp. 247–248).

Life-threatening situations—"a serious threat to one's life or physical integrity" (p. 247)—are a common stimulus of trauma. A serious threat to an individual's sense of self is similarly traumatic. The disintegration of the self is a terrifying experience: one is disconnected not only from significant others and the community, but also from one's own identity. The result is a kind of inner death.

People suffering from PTSD commonly reexperience the traumatic event over and over, although they also display a numbing of general responsiveness and an attempt to avoid stimuli associated with the trauma. The memory is frequently so vivid that the person feels as if he or she is actually living through the event again. Poor concentration, nightmares about the event, and difficulty falling or staying asleep are other symptoms. Emotionally abused clients report the same kind of problems with concentration, constantly recurring images and memories, and sleep disturbances. Even victims who have no clear recognition that they are emotionally abused are fully conscious of the trauma symptoms.

Acknowledgment of the symptoms, however, may occur only if the therapist asks specifically about each one. In many cases the fear of being "crazy" or "losing it" prevents the victim from volunteering the information. Although she initially presented in therapy with somatic problems, Rhonda was able to acknowledge her trauma symptoms when questioned by the therapist.

> It confuses me over and over when one of my mistakes, like burning the rolls, makes Ralph say he wishes we weren't married. It's like being hit with his words about my stupidity, over and over. "What happened?" I wonder. I have nightmares and wake up and can't stop thinking about the conversation, like it's happening all over again. I feel crazy when I hear his voice saying that I'm stupid. I can't concentrate on my schoolwork and avoid going to sleep, because I always think about it when I'm trying to doze off.

Like other trauma victims, emotionally assaulted women often recall details of emotional attacks in vivid and frightening detail. Since the 1970s the intense flashbacks suffered by Vietnam veterans have been explored by a number of researchers. Both just after returning home and for years thereafter, some veterans have had flashbacks of combat situations so real that they believe the attack is happening again. They may strike out in fear and attempt to protect themselves from the imagined enemy. Their trauma has been a challenge for therapeutic intervention and raises questions about how society should deal with flashbacks that lead to violent behavior.

David Niles (1992b) is both a therapist and a Vietnam veteran who has described what it is like to experience combat trauma and its resulting flashbacks. After returning home from a tour of duty in Vietnam, he was hospitalized. From the hospital he called the governor of his state to report that he was a prisoner of war and in danger; then he tore the telephone off the wall. Niles had no memory of this behavior until he was told about it.

In an emotional abuse flashback, the victim is not severed from present reality like the veteran in this example. In addition, she may reexperience the traumatic event at major or minor levels of overtness, which differ from each other somewhat as a grand mal differs from a petit mal seizure. During a minor flashback, an individual often stares into space momentarily while reexperiencing the abusive episode. This replay of emotional abuse can be triggered by thinking about or describing a severely traumatic incident. A victim of emotional abuse experiences both types of flashbacks as real—alive in the present—and outside her control. At the same time, she is also aware of her current situation and, if asked, can usually report that she is reliving an experience. In both types of flashbacks she can hear the therapist's reassurances, although they are not likely to stop the flashback.

Both types are accompanied by fear and anxiety. Because a minor flashback does not precipitate screaming or other overt reactions, however, it may go unrecognized by victims and therapists. Although equally as intense as a major flashback, the inner pain of a minor flashback is likely to be expressed differently—as somatic symptoms, suicidal ideation, despair, loneliness and sadness, and such self-destructive behaviors as eating disorders, substance abuse, and self-mutilation.

Barbara, an attorney who was emotionally abused during her seven-year marriage to John, described what it was like to experience a flashback:

> Sometimes when he wasn't there, I would hear his voice yelling at me, calling me a "whore" and accusing me of sleeping around. I knew he wasn't there and that his voice wasn't really there, either. But that awful taunting and his saying how bad I was kept swirling around in my head, like it was happening all over again, and I'd start to sweat. I felt such pain, and sometimes it would grab me without my even knowing it—I'd just feel all this pain.

Victims of trauma are also prey to intrusive thoughts that are as haunting, repetitive, and outside their control as flashbacks. An emotional abuse victim may ask herself over and over, "Was what I did really as selfish as he says?" or, "Am I really so mean and inadequate?" Even when she is indignant about the criticism and thinks repeatedly that "he shouldn't have spoken to me like that," there is an overriding tone of confusion, a struggle to identify how changing her own behavior might have changed the outcome. The victim's low self-esteem is reflected in her conviction of her own inadequacy and her continuing wish to be attached to the abuser.

Similar persistently painful memories may precipitate flashbacks or intrusive thoughts in which the victim attempts to sort through the abuser's negative labeling, discounts, and negation. When, as often happens, the abuser denies the remembered abuse and projects the blame for their problems onto her, the victim becomes even more confused about her own responsibility for their conflict.

Nightmares focused on current emotional abuse, abusive incidents in earlier adult relationships, or even childhood memories of emotional, physical, and/or sexual abuse are trauma-related symptoms of many forms of violence. Feelings of profound sadness and fear often accompany the nightmares, which frequently contain themes of abandonment and loss of control.

In emotional abuse a phenomenon known as *flooding* can occur when flashbacks, intrusive thoughts, or painful memories—or a combination of all three—overwhelm the victim's thinking. Most often, flooding focuses on threats to the integrity of the victim's self and values, including replays of the mechanisms of overt and covert abuse described in Chapter 1. During flooding, memories and thoughts swirl through the victim's mind with a ferocity and tenacity that can impair judgment and other cognitive functioning. The experience in effect retraumatizes the victim, adding to her confusion and feelings of helplessness. Flooding victims are often involved in automobile accidents caused by their failure to heed stop signs and red lights.

In the past, this accident-prone behavior has usually been attributed to *dissociation*. Its primary dynamic, however, is flooding. It is essential to make a clear distinction between the two phenomena. In the recent literature, dissociation has been studied as a traumatic response of children who have been physically or sexually abused:

Dissociation as a response to trauma . . . always seems to be a response to traumatic life events. Memories and feelings connected with the trauma are forgotten and return as intrusive recollections, feeling states

(such as overwhelming anxiety and panic unwarranted by current experience), fugues, delusions, states of depersonalization, and finally in
behavioral reenactments. (van der Kolk, 1987, p. 185)

The dissociative process is described in DSM-III-R (APA, 1987) as

a disturbance or alteration in the normally integrative functions of
identity, memory, or consciousness . . . the person's customary identity
is temporarily forgotten, and a new identity may be assumed or im-
posed . . . or the customary feeling of one's own reality is lost and is re-
placed by a feeling of unreality . . . important personal events cannot
be recalled. (p. 269)

In child abuse the violation may be so severe that memories of it
are repressed altogether. Later, as an adult, the same person may
react with anxiety and depression when a smell, sight, or the experience of being yelled at brings back the feelings induced by the
original abuse. Even then, the victim usually does not remember
the actual events.

Occasionally a victim of adult emotional abuse displays some
symptoms of dissociation. One victim, for example, acknowledged
during therapy that she did not remember her father's violent rages
even though she trembled and stared off into space while her husband shouted at her. When certain smells, sights, and sounds are reminders of an emotionally abusive event, they can trigger additional trauma. For the most part, however, the primary source of
intrusive imagery in adult emotional abuse is an inner mechanism—flooding by flashbacks and/or intrusive thoughts that vividly
and consciously recall recent events in the present relationship.

It could also be argued that what emotionally abused women experience during flashbacks are hallucinations, which implies pathology on the part of these victims. It is more accurate, however, to
view these phenomena as normal reactions to extreme emotional
stress; that is, a traumatic response to reliving cruel and sadistic
treatment. This view of traumatic responses to emotional abuse is in
keeping with the description by Herman (1992) of the violent stressors that evoke traumatic responses as "extraordinary, not because
they occur rarely, but rather because they overwhelm the ordinary
human adaptations to life. Unlike commonplace misfortunes, trau-

matic events usually involve threats to life or bodily integrity, or a close personal encounter with violence and death (p. 33)."

In emotional abuse, the "close personal encounter with violence" includes overt and covert mechanisms and levels of abuse that threaten to diminish and destroy the self. They are also "extraordinary, not because they occur rarely," but rather because these mechanisms and levels of abuse "overwhelm the ordinary human adaptations to life." The continuous pattern of emotional abuse—unlike the cycle of violence in physical battering—increases the risk of losing the sense of self. Together with the intense yearning for attachment discussed in Chapter 3 and the abuser's abrupt disconnections and threats of abandonment, these extraordinary and overwhelming stressors evoke traumatic reactions.

Diagnosing the Trauma of Emotional Abuse

The symptoms of emotional abuse discussed above—flashbacks, painful memories, nightmares, intrusive imagery, and flooding—frequently gain in their ability to produce trauma by occurring in combination. To a greater or lesser extent they are also symptoms of trauma resulting from other extraordinarily painful experiences. Certain other traumatic responses and patterns of mistreatment, however, are specific to various forms of abuse. In this section I will explore four of the latter—ritualistic emotional abuse, traumatic bonding, the victim-perpetrator syndrome, and psychogenic amnesia—in some detail as I consider some of the difficulties encountered in diagnosing emotional abuse.

Ritualistic Abuse

I have noted in earlier chapters that much emotional abuse has a sort of scriptlike aspect—a patterned repetition of certain abusive mechanisms and behaviors. Full-blown ritualistic emotional abuse carries this tendency much further. It resembles satanism and ritual physical abuse in that (1) it is a concerted attack on the victim's sense of herself, and (2) it involves enactment of a ritual identifying the victim in some way evil. Certain especially painful parts of the ritual are repeated again and again.

Ritualistic abuse frequently causes the victim to experience major flashbacks. During therapy Joanie was describing a repeated form of ritualized abuse in which her husband stomped to the bathroom door when she locked herself inside. Each time he unscrewed the lock mechanism, took off the deadbolt lock, and removed the door from its hinges while taunting her with threats of burning her with a cigarette. He entered the bathroom laughing and brandishing a gun, sometimes holding it to her head. While describing one of these incidents, she suddenly shouted, "No, no, don't hurt me. Leave me alone." She stared at the wall behind the therapist and repeated the plea several times, weeping. The therapist interjected reassurances—"I'm here, I'm here with you"—over and over again. Later Joanie remembered the flashback and said she had been aware that it was not really happening. But reliving the trauma "seemed so real that I spoke out." She also reported that she had heard the therapist's support and was comforted by it.

These flashbacks—and their accompanying exhaustion, confusion, sadness, and fear—leave the victim vulnerable to intrusive thoughts, nightmares, and painful memories as well as to repeated experiences of ritualistic abuse. Thus there is a Dual Cycle of Emotional Abuse in which the ritual and its accompanying terror result in increased susceptability to intrusive imagery. At the same time, the cycle moves in the opposite direction: the intrusive imagery leads to further exhaustion and confusion, resulting in enhanced vulnerability to the experience of ritualistic emotional abuse (see Figure 1).

Like the perpetrators of satanic abuse and cult rituals, the emotional abuser endeavors to reform the thoughts of the victim through "fluctuation of assault and leniency" and "an assault on identity" (Lifton, 1961, pp. 67–72). Focusing his torture on the victim's supposedly evil character, he confuses and dissolves her trust in her own senses and assumptions about how the world works (Sakheim & Devine, 1992). For example, when Tina became the target of Jeff's identity attacks, he first forced her to watch pornographic films in which the woman was mutilated and animals were injured. He followed them with insults about her ugly and inherently "disgusting body" and threats of various kinds of sexual torture. His threat to burn her with cigarettes while she lay naked were usually sufficient to traumatize Tina, who would cry while

Figure 1.
The Dual Cycle of Ritualistic Emotional Abuse

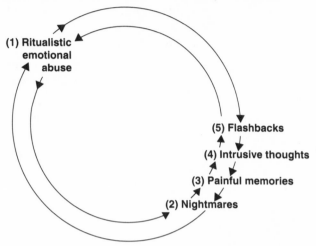

Jeff laughed and assured her that he would "do all the thinking in the family." He would then order her to lick the floor, slap her own "dirty mouth," and force her to watch him hit the dog.

Establishment of guilt in the victim, another characteristic mechanism of satanic and ritualistic abuse of children, is often used by emotional abusers, too. Victims are forced "to commit atrocities by the adults in the group who would then point out how evil the child must have been to have done these things" (Katchen & Sakheim, 1992, p. 31). Tina described being forced to watch helplessly while her dog was injured as "so atrocious, horrifying, and degrading because I was committing a terrible deed by watching and not stopping the cruelty. Then he would criticize me for letting the dog get hurt."

As in cult ritualistic torture, the emotional abuser often threatens that the woman will bear the responsibility if a significant other (a parent, child, or pet) is injured as a result of her behavior. Jeff used this method of inducing obedience by threatening to blow up Tina's parents' home if she left him. He would add that their deaths would be Tina's fault.

Another crucial aspect of ritualized emotional abuse, self-betrayal, seriously undermines the victim's sense of self. In cult abuse a victim is often forced to show disrespect toward a religious symbol

(Lifton, 1961). In the same way, the emotional abuse victim is forced to perform abhorrent or disgusting acts or behaviors that betray her most cherished values. Jeff threatened Tina that he would lock her outside the house without her clothes unless she engaged in sexual practices that she regarded as "shameful and dirty."

Just as a cult-abused child may be forced to desecrate and denounce the symbols of the church, the emotional abuse victim finds herself losing treasured symbols of her selfhood. Tina described Jeff's assault on the quick thinking and logical ability that were, for her, symbols of her intelligence. He threatened to abandon her unless she complied with a confession ritual; for hours on end he supplied the words and forced her to repeat admissions of "stupidity" and "sexual perversion."

All these intrusive forms of coercion preclude independent thinking and clear judgment on the part of the victim. In cult abuse the victim encounters a "Kafka-like maze of vague and yet damning accusations: he could neither understand exactly what he was guilty of . . . nor could he in any way establish his innocence. [He was] overwhelmed by fatigue, confusion, and helplessness" (Lifton, 1961, p. 70). In ritualized emotional abuse, too, the hostagelike experience of mind control and brainwashing leads the victim to internalize the abuser's degraded images of herself and to accede to his accusations. When Jeff repeatedly accused her of having affairs, feeling no respect for him, not loving him, and so on, Tina was completely bewildered. She could not establish her innocence to his satisfaction, "so I gave up, [and] felt confused, exhausted, and helpless."

The cases of ritualized emotional abuse cited above employed highly aggressive, overt mechanisms of coercive abuse. Yet although some abusers use more subtle, covert forms of abuse, the ritualized pattern of abuse is the same; the abuser's oft-repeated sequence of behavior results in the victim's panic and trauma (as, for example, in the case of Terry and Albert described in Chapter 1). Perceiving herself as incapable of escaping from or changing the situation, the victim is an emotional hostage, overwhelmed and helpless. As Tina acknowledged:

I may be a sharp lawyer, but I can't think when this happens. My confusion and some kind of falling apart, actual destruction of what I think of as myself, kick in and there I am, participating in this incredible ritual yet another time. I feel like less of a human being.

The abuser's continuous, degrading comments, insults, and projections of blame diminish the victim's sense of self. Futile attempts to flail out verbally in self-defense run up against the abuser's denial of accountability and projection of blame onto the victim. At this point, frustrated and despairing, some victims flail out physically—pushing or striking the abuser, or waving a gun or a knife—in an effort to protect the disintegrating self. Amidst the chaos and confusion, the components that make up the cohesive self are separated and unavailable to the victim. Tina reported this sense of

lostness, like the parts of me were scattered about like ashes after a cremation. Yet in time they came back together, and I could think again. I always avoided Jeff before a big trial, because I was scared to go into court paralyzed emotionally, destroyed for how long I never knew.

Traumatic Bonding

This loss of self leaves the victim vulnerable to traumatic bonding, a type of attachment that intensifies the loss of selfhood and makes reintegrating the identify even more difficult. Fear and terror render the emotionally abused woman incapable of detaching herself from the relationship with the abuser, for she has no separate and cohesive self to detach. The traumatic bond is an incredibly strong one.

Traumatic bonding in emotional abuse is similar to a form of attachment known as the *Stockholm syndrome*, a model based on the paradoxical psychosocial responses of hostages to their captors. It was found that hostages develop a genuine fondness for their captors when the latter use a method of control that alternates terror with kindness. This mixture results in a power imbalance (Graham, Rawlings, & Rimini, 1988) that renders hostages dependent on their captors for emotional as well as physical needs. Patty Hearst was kidnapped by the Symbionese Liberation Army and she was first imprisoned in a locked closet (Hearst & Moscow, 1982). When she expressed political agreement with her captors they allowed her to spend more time out of the closet. Although blindfolded, she could eat with her captors and attend meetings with them. She depended on these captors for survival, both in a positive sense (for feeding her) and in a negative sense (for not killing her. The resulting traumatic attachment produced her efforts to please her captors in various ways—for example, by taking on a new name and a revolutionary identity—and thus maintain her hopes for survival.

Symonds (1975) explains the paradox of the hostage–captor situation as resulting from an "overwhelming terror . . . [that] causes clinging, nonthinking behavior; he clings to the very person who has placed him in danger" (p. 22). He compares the hostage's traumatic bonding with the captor to the response of victims who voluntarily remain with a powerful criminal who is terrorizing them: "The fright response of victims is usually a frozen, frightened reaction. The reaction of fear is so profound and overwhelming that the victim feels hopeless about getting away. All hope of survival is dependent on appeasing the criminal" (p. 22).

This traumatic bonding occurs in an intimate relationship when one partner alternates between positive, kindly responses and negative, abusive reactions (Dutton & Painter, 1981). In the cycle of violence that occurs with physical battering, both the abuse and the kindness are intermittent (Walker, 1984a). The batterer builds up tension, explodes with violence, and then apologizes and is quiescent during a "honeymoon" period (Walker, 1979, 1984a). In emotional abuse, however, traumatic bonding and desperate clinging are created by a continuous pattern of abuse marked by intermittent warmth and abrupt disconnection. The overall tone of the relationship is abusive and is occasionally relieved by moments of affection and empathy.

The traumatic bond is difficult to break, in great part because emotional abuse victims rarely perceive this ongoing bonding process and its effect on them. When they begin to understand (1) the inconsistency of the warmth in the connection, (2) the rarity of these moments of connection, and (3) the harshness and brutality of the disconnections, they have experienced an important insight. Even then, however, their damaged sense of self usually precludes immediate separation from the abuser. Only when they have developed a more integrated sense of themselves and reestablished connectedness with other individuals and a supportive community can they approach that important step.

Victim-Perpetrators

During the victim's intense and painful struggle for connection, she may become a victim-perpetrator. As explained in earlier chapters, a victim-perpetrator is a physically and/or emotionally abused woman who engages in illegal activity as a consequence of the abuse. Both the traumatic bonding and the destruction of the self contribute to her blind obedience. Many victim-perpetrators report feeling that they are "coming apart" during an episode of emotional abuse; they are flooded with confusion and emptiness. Experiencing this loss of self, they also lose their ability to make decisions and panic at the idea of being abandoned. Their confused thoughts and desperate need for connection render them unable to remove themselves from the abusive situation and the criminal activities of the partner.

In Chapter 1 I described how Barb unknowingly bought ingredients for three bombs and delivered the packages to the post office when her husband, Tony, ordered her to do so. Later, under questioning, Tony acknowledged that he had not told Barb what was in the packages. She had asked once, but he had ordered her never to ask again, so she did not. Barb and Tony were charged with the murder of three businessmen killed by the bombs.

I first saw Barb when she was referred for a psychosocial evaluation. She was out on bond and wearing an ankle bracelet that enabled authorities to monitor her movements. The emaciated thirty-eight-year-old woman stared at me, hanging her head and answering my questions in a whisper. Her long blond hair hung about her face like an unopened curtain. She expressed horror at her part in the murders, wondering over and over how she could have participated. At other times, she remained silent for long periods.

She lived with her sister, who complained that Barb ate very little. When I discovered that she liked health food, I began bringing a selection of health foods to our sessions. Barb described this sharing of food as "nurturing" and began to talk about her relationship with Tony.

> Tony was warm to me sometimes but was always critical and demeaning. When he threatened to leave I'd do anything he said. He called me "whore" and "bitch" and said I was selfish and mean. I felt confused and

scared. And when he'd start to leave, I'd beg him to stay. Sometimes he wouldn't talk to me for days at a time, and I would begin to feel unsure of who I was or what I was like. It felt like I was coming apart at the seams, and I could hardly think. I was broken up into parts, and I didn't know how to fit them back together. I did whatever he told me to so he'd be warm and wouldn't leave.

Barb followed Tony's orders, one by one, without recognizing what he intended to do. The feelings of disintegration she experienced prevented her from analyzing the situation or using her own moral judgment. The traumatic bond with Tony made her, in effect, a hostage. His threats of abandonment were coercive and controlling, and she believed that she had no choice but to follow his orders.

The role of a traumatized victim-perpetrator is difficult for individuals in the court system to understand. For Julia, whose relationship with Tim was marked by constant emotional abuse and only intermittent warmth, the choice must have seemed clear. He ordered her to sit in the car while he robbed a bank at gunpoint: "He told me if I drove away, he'd come by and do a drive-by shooting and kill my two children." Since they lived in an area where there had been a number of deaths from drive-by shootings, Julia believed him and obeyed his orders.

Whether serving as a psychosocial evaluator prior to a criminal trial or treating private clients, therapists need to be able to diagnose severe emotional abuse that results in PTSD and traumatic bonding. Unfortunately, diagnosis is often complicated by the apparent similarity between trauma symptomatology and other types of psychosocial distress. The presenting symptoms of emotionally abused women have been mistaken for those characteristic of personality disorders, schizophrenia, and seizure disorders in which "a psychodynamically determined dissociative episode occurs" (Hammond, 1989, p. 91).

In addition, emotionally abused women often suffer from various somatic symptoms that are easily misdiagnosed. Headaches and upper respiratory illnesses are common metaphors for pressure, inner crying, and despair. Victims often report aching in various parts of the body that resembles tendonitis or arthritis. Many emotionally abused women suffer from bladder discomfort and infections and report a crisis in trust that explains the underlying metaphor: Should they "let go" and share their unhappiness in an effort to connect, or "hold in" expressions of feeling that usually lead to debasement?

Herman (1992) suggests that therapists need a clearer understanding of the relationship between psychopathology and abuse: "Instead of conceptualizing the psychopathology of the victim as a response to an abusive situation, mental health professionals have frequently attributed the abusive situation to the victim's presumed underlying pathology" (p. 116). She attributes the misdiagnosis of trauma victims to a lack of understanding of trauma itself:

> Concepts of personality organization developed under normal circumstances are applied to victims, without any understanding of the corrosion of personality that occurs under conditions of prolonged terror. Thus, patients who suffer from the complex aftereffects of chronic trauma still commonly risk being misdiagnosed as having personality disorders. (p. 117)

Diagnosis of the victim-perpetrator and of other emotional abuse victims has yielded considerable documentation of the effects of ongoing severe trauma. Traumatic bonding and the pervasive terror of the victim is not provoked by one traumatic event but by repeated emotional stresses. It is difficult to capture this emotional-hostage phenomenon with the diagnostic categories currently available.

Herman (1992) has argued that a more complex category is needed to differentiate the prolonged terror experienced by some trauma victims from the time-limited traumatic events usually seen as responsible for PTSD. Her proposed category would convey the traumatic effects of (1) living in captivity and (2) current experiences of abuse. Because most victims of emotional abuse are currently living in abusive situations, such a category would enable therapists to assess such ongoing stressors as continuous verbal aggression and threats to harm or kill the victim.

It would thus recognize the severe trauma resulting from threats to destruction of the sense of self in cases of emotional abuse. Ewing's analysis of the impact of such threats in the context of family violence is relevant here. Arguing on behalf of abused women who kill their batterers, he suggests that the legal defense of self-defense should encompass psychological as well as physical defense:

> But what of those, perhaps the majority of battered homicide defendants, who kill not to avert an imminent threat of death or serious physical injury but rather to protect themselves from the infliction of extremely serious psychological injury—those who kill in what has been called psychological self-defense (Ewing, 1987, p. 77)

Ewing (1990) defines the self as the "psychological functions, attributes, processes, and dimensions of experience that give meaning and value to physical existence" (p. 586). More than just physical existence, it also encompasses the "mental being and thus includes such recognized and socially valued psychological attributes as security, autonomy, identity, consciousness, and spirituality" (p. 586).

Reviewing one hundred cases of women who killed their batterers, Ewing (1987) found that nearly all of them had also experienced "severe psychological abuse," including threats of death or mutilation, the killing of family pets, and abuse of and threats to harm or kill the children (p. 32). In cases marked by these forms of emotional abuse, the woman's fear that her sense of self was disintegrating usually preceded the murder.

This threatened or actual injury to the self from emotional abuse is found in other types of trauma as well. Herman (1992) has described how trauma damages the basic personality structure of its victims: "They lose their trust in themselves, in other people, and in God. Their self-esteem is assaulted by experiences of humiliation, guilt, and helplessness. . . . The identity they have formed prior to the trauma is irrevocably destroyed" (p. 56).

Psychogenic Amnesia

They may also suffer from psychogenic amnesia, an inability to recall specific aspects of a traumatic event. While most emotional abuse victims recall abusive incidents in vivid and comprehensive detail, some have psychogenic amnesia about an especially terrifying component of the experience. This type of trauma may result from (1) multiple forms of emotional abuse, including death threats; (2) the belief that physical and emotional death is imminent; and (3) the perception that escape is impossible. When both emotional and physical abuse are present prior to a murder, it is emotional abuse that most often directly precedes it.

The partial loss of memory means that the victim may not recall what happened for periods of time during the murder incident. "The gun went off" is the typical description of a victim who has struck out in terror after being threatened; she may not remember pulling the trigger. Just before and after the memory lapse, events often seem to move in fast or slow motion. Frequently a victim reports feeling depersonalized and distant prior to or after the murder. She may feel as if she is floating on the ceiling, watching the drama unfold below.

Julie was frightened of Troy throughout their ten-year marriage. As she had grown up fearing both her parents, this was not a new type of intimate attachment for her. Troy often controlled her by threatening to hurt her dog and by withdrawing his affections for long periods of time.

> Troy said I wasn't worth anything. I felt like nothing inside. I was so lonely and frightened. When I tried to hug him or be close, he would be cold and seem to be thinking about other things. Sometimes he held the dog under his arm and punched her. He called me stupid and ugly and put me down in front of our friends. I felt dead. And then one night, he said he'd kill me. When he came toward me, I picked up a pair of scissors and waved it around. And then I can't remember what happened. I didn't even know I'd cut him on the neck. I called the ambulance. When they got there, he was dead and they called the police.

Flailing out with a knife or gun is a characteristic response of an emotionally abused woman in a traumatic situation. The flailing may be verbal or physical and is a random series of movements or verbalizations intended as self-defense. They may lead to additional abuse or, as in Julie's case, result in the abuser's death.

Browne (1989, p. 107) also views emotional abuse as a contributing factor when battered women kill. She sees their despair, terror, and overwhelming sense of entrapment as the cumulative result of the repeated physical and mental assaults they have undergone. As noted in Chapter 3, this desperation engenders the profound loneliness and sadness characteristic of the traumatized, emotionally abused woman. She is cut off from the warmth of her friends and family by the abuser's jealousy and attempts to isolate her, and she is disconnected by his abuse from her own self. His inconsistent empathic sharing and withdrawals of warmth may take the form of covert or explicit threats to abandon her.

The threat of abandonment or actual withdrawal from a relationship is a potent mechanism of abuse that can lead to trauma. The typical abuser moves in and out of closeness with the victim as it meets his needs. He may disconnect from her as a means of punishment or manipulation, but sometimes he does so simply because his attention is directed elsewhere. He may not even recognize the impact his disconnections have on her. Frequently, in fact, he lacks full awareness of the victim as a separate individual with different needs and wishes. He is likely to project his own feelings and perceptions of the world onto her. If he fears losing his partner, for example, he may accuse her of having an affair with another man.

Most emotional abuse victims are not aware of the depth of their own despair, sadness, and fear until these are revealed in the therapeutic setting. They almost always focus the blame for problems in the relationship on themselves. Suicidal ideation, a common symptom among victims, is the ultimate form of self-blame and internalized self-annihilation.

In addition, they often suffer from periodic episodes of confusion and disintegration stemming from the covert mechanisms of emotional abuse. Jen, a thirty-two-year-old restaurant owner, initially presented for therapy with symptoms of depression and low self-esteem. A battery of medical tests had failed to uncover any physical causes for the painful chest pains and stomachaches she was suffering, and she felt desperate and confused: "I don't know what's wrong with me. I'm scared and confused all the time. And I worry about doing well in my restaurant business. My husband Peter has invested a lot of money in it. I always seem to let him down. Sometimes I think I'd be better off dead."

A joint interview with the couple, who had been married for seven years, revealed Peter's continuous put-downs and discounting of his wife's abilities. When she reacted to them with tears, he denied saying anything hurtful and accused her of being oversensitive. During individual therapy sessions, when Jen recounted examples of Peter's numerous threats to abandon her, she was unaware that they had traumatized her and resulted in psychic amnesia.

> Peter loves me, but he sometimes accuses me of being selfish and purposefully demeaning to him. I never mean to, and I feel confused when he says that. I go through what I have said and try to figure out how I could be more tactful. I've had two car accidents while thinking over and over about his accusations. Sometimes I feel like I don't even exist. I feel empty inside, like a lousy wife, just plain dead inside, like I should kill myself and finish the job. Sometimes when I am the most scared, I think so hard that I forget what I have said or done.

Another victim of a husband's periodic threats of abandonment was Mattie, a forty-eight-year-old accountant. She had been married to Jake for twelve years. He frequently called her "bitch" and "whore" and depicted her as an inadequate mother. When he threatened to leave her, Mattie experienced terrible loneliness. Painful memories of his accusations and intrusive thoughts interfered with her concentration on her work.

> He says I am a lousy mother. I try to be a good mother, but he says I'm insensitive and cruel to our daughter. He always has lots of examples, and it takes me hours to go through them and figure out where he has exaggerated and if I have been OK. I know I drink too much, but it makes me hurt less. My friends say I'm a good mother, but I don't see them much. When I'm trying to concentrate at work, I keep thinking about his saying he'll leave me.

An emotionally abused woman who fears abandonment usually responds by trying to mollify her partner, perhaps by repressing her own opinions or giving up important personal preferences and values. The abusive relationship leaves little room for individual differences; the abuser's many rigid rules and expectations are designed to meet only *his* needs. For the victim, the likely result of this self-suppression is a further deterioration in her sense of connection to herself.

Another characteristic of this victim is her repeated effort to master the trauma of emotional assault by understanding it and changing herself. She feels simultaneously hopeless about attaining a warm and empathic connection with the partner and convinced that she can achieve it by changing her own behavior. She may spend a great deal of time analyzing each new emotional attack in search of the understanding that will enable her to create change. Focused on her own behavior, she is unable to perceive the overall pattern of abuse that underlies all the separate incidents.

When, in therapy, she begins to connect her feelings of confusion, desperation, and loss of self to these incidents, she will need to reveal the details of multiple assaults. Her painful memories may engender flooding, intrusive and uncontrollable thoughts, and frightening flashbacks. For the therapist, though, being in the presence of an emotional abuse victim experiencing a major or minor flashback may be very difficult. The outpouring of descriptions of cruelty, sadism, and violence can lead to secondary trauma—what McCann and Pearlman (1990b) call "traumatic countertransference" or "vicarious traumatization." Nausea, extreme discomfort, difficulty sleeping, and intrusive thoughts are not unusual symptoms among therapists working with trauma victims. A patient's accounts or images reminiscent of the therapist's own past can revive still-painful traumatic memories. One therapist reported having nightmares that reflected the ongoing emotional degradation of her client, including feelings of abandonment. We need to be aware, as Herman (1992) points out, that "trauma is contagious. In the role of witness to disaster or atrocity, the therapist at times is emotionally overwhelmed. She experiences, to a lesser degree, the same terror, rage, and despair as the patient" (p. 140). The support of colleagues is crucial in these situations.

In the chapter about a new model of therapy (Chapter 6), the use of flashbacks will be described in a therapeutic technique called "retrospective flashback recall." The therapist's own secondary trauma may be evident during this process.

I have argued in this chapter that emotional abuse leads to PTSD and that therapists, advocates, and theorists working with emotionally abused women need to recognize them as victims of trauma. Herman's critique of the inadequate diagnostic perspectives for trauma victims helps explain why this remains a problem. Another obstacle to helping victims of emotional abuse can be the theoretical perspective employed by the therapist. Many clinicians utilize the same theoretical basis for establishing a diagnosis and treatment modality; when the client is a victim of emotional abuse, however, this method may not be effective. In Chapter 5, I explore why the therapy must first focus on the abusive process, reintegration of the self, and establishment of nonabusive connections and emotional safety before moving on to issues of growth and self-realization.

5

Theoretical Perspectives

Therapists, advocates, and theorists looking at the problem of emotional and physical abuse embrace a wide range of different theoretical perspectives on which they base assessment and intervention plans. For example, a therapist espousing the codependency model is likely to diagnose an abused woman as caught in a dysfunctional relationship from which she needs to detach. A therapist oriented toward social learning theory, in contrast, may explain family violence by focusing on learned violent behaviors.

In the early stages of therapy, neither of these orientations is likely to be helpful to the victim of emotional abuse. For this client, the initial focus must be on the abusive process, reintegration of the self, establishment of nonabusive connections, and emotional safety. Once these crucial issues are resolved, various treatment modalities can be useful in fostering other types of growth.

Codependency

When Andrea came to her first therapy session with me, she apologized repeatedly for not having left her emotionally abusive boyfriend.

> My therapist said I am codependent and should detach. I was supposed to leave Frank and enter into the twelve-step program to break my addiction. I feel like a failure, 'cause I couldn't accomplish this during the

eight months I was in therapy. I went to a few step meetings, but didn't go back. Sometimes I can hear Frank yelling at me when he isn't even here. I feel so lost and confused.

Andrea was unable to detach from the relationship. The emotional abuse she experienced had so diminished her sense of self that there was not enough left to enable her to pull away. The therapist who urged her to separate from her abusive lover assumed that there would still be a self entity after she left him. For an emotionally abused woman, however, this assumption is not initially valid. Disconnected from both her self and the community, the traumatized victim feels that she has no choice but to cling desperately to the partner, no matter how abusive he is.

Porterfield (1989) who utilizes the codependency model, accurately describes the effects of emotional abuse: "Mental degradation, name-calling and putdowns . . . chip away at our self-esteem if we hear them often enough, especially from someone who knows us well and who claims to love us" (p. 10). Moreover, she recognizes that "these insults etch their way into our thinking until they become our reality. We put ourselves down with his phrases even when he's not around. . . . We deny our worth as human beings" (p. 11). She also acknowledges that emotionally abused women can suffer from Post-Traumatic Stress Disorder (PTSD).

Nonetheless, Porterfield expects these victims to take charge of their own lives, realize that they can give up patterns of behavior stemming from childhood, and leave the abusive relationship. A victim cannot, however, reject emotional abuse that she does not recognize. Porterfield's assumption that emotionally abused women will see themselves as abused fails to allow for their tendency to internalize blame and to suffer from depression, confusion, and anxious attachment. Her codependency model also misses the hostage-like emotional captivity that is so characteristic of emotional abuse.

At the same time, Porterfield's identification of the key characteristics of the emotional abuser—such as denial of responsibility for the woman's feelings, and accusations that she has misinterpreted him and put words in his mouth (p. 10)—are very much on target. She points to the inconsistency of the abuser's criticisms, to the fact that "nothing is spared his disapproval," and to his use of hyperbole: "She *always* says the wrong thing" (p. 11). She notes that "the man who would never threaten to bash his boss's brains in with a heavy glass ashtray feels perfectly at ease verbalizing that threat to his wife if she comes home five minutes late" (p. 2). This "emotional coward" justifies his "reign of terror" (p. 3) on the grounds that his spouse forces him into rage and sarcasm. Porterfield's account also recognizes that his unpredictable behavior, sometimes loving and sometimes furiously angry, forges an intense bond with his victim, causing her to "cling to the false hope" that he is changing (p. 4).

Her description of this kind of bonding, however, is based on the cyclic pattern of physical battering, rather than the continuous model of emotional abuse. The emotional abuser, as noted earlier, expresses his rage in a constant stream of overt or covert abuse, infusing only intermittent bits of kindness and warmth into the relationship. The bond is not only intense, it is traumatic and hostage-like; the reign of terror encircles the diminished victim, who sees no way to attain emotional safety outside it.

Social Learning Perspective

Another perspective used by therapists working with these clients focuses on the social and cultural environment. These therapists point to social conditions as the root cause of family violence:

> Men who assault . . . have done so, often for many years, with complete immunity. Most men who abuse their partners believe that it is justifiable and appropriate. Women brought up in the same atmosphere share these beliefs. Societally and culturally, abuse of women has been condoned and sanctioned as men abuse their power to control what they believe to be theirs. (Frank & Golden, 1992, pp. 5–6)

Arguing from this perspective, Pence (1985) holds—contrary to the view of many therapists that the low self-esteem of physically abused women is a *cause* of their involvement in a battering relationship—that their low self-esteem is a *result* of the abuse they have suffered (that is, that it is a learned response). It is probable that both processes contribute to the situation. A history of abuse does render the victim especially vulnerable to demeaning treatment at the hands of a loved one; and the experience of repeated emotional and/or physical abuse in adulthood does diminish the victim's sense of worth, even if she has no childhood history of abuse.

Most adult victims of emotional abuse, however, do recall being emotionally abused in childhood. Even victims who believe they were not abused sometimes report family relations markedly lacking in expressiveness and emotional bonding. Their later vulnerability may be based less on an abusive history than on their early caregivers' lack of warmth, empathy, and responsiveness to the child's needs. While some of these victims may simply be unaware of the actual emotional abuse they suffered in childhood, others may not have suffered any.

Social learning therapists and advocates focus less on this individual and family level, however, and more on the messages broadcast by an oppressive and violent society. They view the growth of the codependency perspective with alarm; using the term *codependency*, they argue, compounds the problem and obscures the reality of a wider system of oppression that sees women's emotional and physical well-being as unimportant (Pence, 1985). They search for solutions to family violence in such social actions as legislative changes, development of shelter resources, and establishment of legal consequences for battering. As with most other perspectives, the focus of attention in social learning theory is on physical abuse.

While this is a valuable perspective for social action, it involves less focus on the immediate needs of traumatized victims of emotional and physical abuse—women who become involved in serial abusive relationships and suffer from anxious attachment and suicidal ideation. To make the transition from victim to survivor, these women need internal changes, an alteration in their individual relationships, and social change.

A variation on this perspective emphasizes the socialization process and cultural influences (Watts & Courtois, 1981). It assumes that "men are socialized to violence" (Scher & Stevens, 1987) through the "heroes and role models provided for boys [that] are also spurs to aggressive behavior" (Gerzon, 1982). Furthermore, because men are socialized not to cry or show their emotions, they are less able to work through painful feelings and more likely to use anger as their primary means of emotional expression (O'Neil, 1981). Since not all men exposed to such cultural influences become violent, however, this perspective fails to explain how these influences make some more likely to become violent than others.

Nonetheless, some of the intervention strategies based on the socialization model are useful for helping abusive men recognize their own pain and become more aware of the effect of their violence on others. It can also assist them in learning other ways to feel good, responsible, and in charge without dominating or humiliating their partners. One program, called Men Stopping Violence (Bathrick, Carlin, Kaufman, & Vodde, 1988), encourages emotionally and physically abusive men to attain their wishes without disparaging the other person. If, for example, a man likes to have dinner at a certain time, and his partner has not yet returned from work, it becomes his responsibility to fix dinner instead of exploding at her when she comes home. The goal of the program is to substitute new skills and techniques of coping with life's problems for attempts to control one's partner through isolation, jealousy, or violence.

In a group context, abusive men—many of whom have been ordered to participate by the courts—learn to discuss the causes of their rage and to find other ways to give vent to it. Ultimately, however, each man is held responsible for identifying the antecedents of his own fury and for not responding to them through anger. The therapist encourages a participant who feels his temper rising to take a "time out" to calm down. When he returns, he learns to discuss the incident in terms that acknowledge his responsibility: "I feel angry about that" is acceptable, while "You are selfish and stupid to have done that" is blaming someone else for his feelings.

The therapist's firmness in pointing out emotionally abusive behavior is especially valuable, as neither partner is fully aware of the emotional abuse process. Helping the abuser understand the historical and current precipitants of his rage is also helpful. The crucial step, however, must always be his acceptance of responsibility for controlling his violence in the present.[1]

---

1. The need to review safety steps and provide escape routes for physically battered women has been widely recognized in the past few years. No similar mapping of safe emotional escape routes seems to be acknowledged for emotionally abused women. Yet these victims are at high risk for suicidal and homicidal behavior. Providing safety plans for victims of emotional abuse is discussed in Chapter 6.

Some therapists and advocates are uncomfortable with psycho-educational methods like those used in Men Stopping Violence. In some cases, they argue, these methods can be used to familiarize the victim with the abusive process and to suggest that she (1) become aware of her own behavior and change it in some way and (2) assist in setting limits for the abuser. When this happens, she is acting in self-defense rather than sending a clear message to the abuser to stop the violence.

Moreover, even after they learn to recognize their violence, many emotionally abusive men acknowledge that their efforts to improve their self-control are only partially successful. A woman who remains in such a relationship must therefore be helped to ensure her own emotional safety through therapeutic techniques that provide a heightened understanding of the process of emotional abuse, her own anxious attachment, and options for disattaching from the abuse process. I present a therapy model aimed at achieving these goals in Chapter 6.

Battered Woman Syndrome

Some therapists' treatment of abuse relies on the description by Walker (1984) of the "battered woman syndrome" among physically abused women. This cluster of characteristics includes low self-esteem, fear of the partner's actual and/or threatened abuse, and *learned helplessness*—a feeling that no alteration or escape from the situation is possible. The concept of learned helplessness is based on the work of Seligman (1975), who observed this helpless condition among animals unable to alter their environments. In his experiments he subjected dogs to random shocks at variable intervals that were completely unrelated to their behavior. Nothing they could do would protect them from the shocks. Under this treatment the dogs became passive and refused to leave their cages as the shocks continued, even though the cage doors eventually were left open.

According to Walker (1984a), learned helplessness explains why physically battered women feel unable to change their situation. Because emotionally abused women also experience learned helplessness, therapeutic interventions that provide opportunities for victims to enhance their sense of personal control are powerful tools. Learning about the emotional abuse process and developing ways of reintegrating the fragmented or diminished self are just such methods of empowerment.

Systems Theory

Another perspective, systemic therapy, depicts family violence as an interactive process between partners locked in a pattern of mutual behavior and responses. Viewing both partners as responsible for the abusive interactions, the therapist works with them to alter their behavior toward each other. Some systemic therapists counsel partners together, even when emotional and/or physical violence is present.

Considerations of safety, however, should preclude holding joint interviews in cases of physical and emotional abuse, except for those few sessions in which a diagnosis is established or an effort is made to control the abuser's violence. Even then, issues of emotional safety must be carefully worked out prior to the joint interview. Otherwise, a therapeutic safe haven for the victim—as important an aspect of therapy as psychosocial growth—cannot be created. (I deal with the structuring of joint interviews in Chapter 6.)

According to systemic therapists, the initial battering incident is rooted in a pattern learned in the past (Lawson, 1989); thereafter the abuse is maintained and made predictable by a system of developing family rules. The pattern develops and continues because it serves a function, such as maintaining the system (Lawson, 1989). Some spouses are described as battered because of their submissive behavior (Everstine & Everstine, 1983), which frustrates the dominant spouse and results in an escalation of violence. As long as one partner continues to be submissive, the other partner's anger will grow.

Explaining the behavior of victims and abusers in terms of interactional dynamics and system stability—as if there were no differentiation of responsibility—is inaccurate; more important, it is wrong. The systemic perspective lacks a clear moral judgment regarding the unacceptability of violence. It not only fails to protect the victim from further abuse, it does not distinguish between blaming her and helping her change her responses to the partner's violence. However useful it may be to understand the root causes of the abuser's behavior and his current emotional dilemma, it is not sufficient. The therapist must firmly assert, to both the abuser and the victim, that it is the abuser who is responsible for the violence and must stop it. In most systemic therapy, though, this firm understanding has not been a major focus of concern, as the following passage illustrates:

> A battering response becomes part of the family's established interactional pattern because it may have served an initial purpose (e.g., tension reduction) and because of the tendency of a system to maintain pattern stability. The escalatory nature of the abusive cycle is maintained by mutual reactions between spouses such that submissiveness by one spouse promotes further assertiveness and hence battering. . . . Attempts to placate and thus please the abusive spouse promote greater escalation and oscillation of violence. (Lawson, 1989, pp. 365–366)

Contrary to this analysis, emotionally abused women do *not* experience tension reduction in an abusive interaction. The abuser is the primary rule-setter and only beneficiary; the mechanisms of abuse are geared solely toward expressing his rage and controlling and diminishing the victim. The abuser will escalate his violence without regard to the victim's behavior. Moreover, systemic theory fails to consider the reactive component of the victim's behavior. Her submission is not acquiescence to a system of violence but an attempt to avoid further abuse and obtain some modicum of validation and warmth.

Another application of the systems perspective explains physical abuse in terms of the abuser's sense of inadequacy and the victim's need to feel that her husband is dependent on her. Feeling inferior to his partner, who is described as behaving in an "overadequate" manner, the abuser uses violence to bring the relationship back into equilibrium. The victim, it is argued, accepts the abuse; her powerlessness is accepted by both parties and serves as a security bond between them (Hoffman, 1981). Hoffman sees this acceptance as the basis of the extraordinary mutual attachment of the physically abusive couple.

A woman does not, however, need to appear overadequate or even adequate to be emotionally abused by her partner. The mechanisms of abuse operate regardless of her achievements or lack of them. Like other explanations of systemic theory, this reasoning makes the victim appear to accept the abuse as a means of sustaining the system. It is inaccurate to say, though, that emotionally abused women actually accept the pain of abuse; in fact, many do not recognize the full extent of the emotional abuse they endure. Moreover, in part because the victim's sense of self is diminished or destroyed, she perceives no escape and unknowingly tolerates the abuse that fosters her traumatic bonding.

Lawson (1989) has suggested a form of therapeutic intervention that applies the varied components of the systems perspective to family violence. His intervention goals include the following:

- Interruption and cessation of the cycle of violence
- Increased acceptance of individual responsibility
- Expanding the couple's options for perceiving their situation and dealing with it
- Differentiating between the needs of the man and the woman
- Reestablishing the equilibrium of the system

He recognizes that it may not at first be possible to achieve the latter three goals "if a high risk for violence exists" (p. 366), and that batterers must first accept full responsibility for their behavior. Nonetheless, he and other system theorists hold to the view that both individuals are responsible for the escalation and maintenance of the abusive system (Cook & Cook, 1984).

Lawson (1989) also suggests that battering often goes undetected because neither spouse presents abuse as a concern in therapy. He therefore points to the need for therapists to explore the possibility of violence during the initial assessment and to elicit information about a couple's ways of dealing with conflict. If abuse is found or suspected, he recommends that the therapist conduct separate interviews to gather further information, focusing his or her attention on the sequence of events immediately preceding and accompanying violent incidents.

Lawson acknowledges the need to protect the abused woman during the initial stages of therapy and to obtain a commitment from the batterer to desist from violence. Although some individual sessions may be called for, he argues that joint interviews should be resumed as soon as safety permits. Other systemic therapists suggest that extended individual sessions may foster the impression of a coalition between the therapist and victim (Rosenbaum & O'Leary, 1986).

Lawson (1989) also contends that painting a picture of the abuser as a "monster" to a spouse who sees him as a loving husband may not be good therapy (p. 369); in fact, it may even stiffen her resolve to stay with him. Accepting the woman's "firmly held view of her husband in order to obtain therapeutic leverage would seem to take precedence over attempting to persuade her of her equality and right to assert herself" (p. 368). He illustrates his strategy with this example of a systems therapist's communication with an abused client:

> Because you do love your husband and you desire to improve your relationship with him, it is necessary to provide each of you with some space in order to make a new start in the relationship that you have indicated you want. I sense that you deeply love your husband and are willing to demonstrate the true depth of your love by giving him the space he needs when the angry pattern begins to escalate. In this way, you ensure that the violent pattern will begin to change and thus preserve your love and commitment to him. (p. 369)

For several reasons, however, such a strategy cannot be effective in a case of emotional abuse. First, a traumatized, anxiously attached, emotionally abused woman would be unable to succeed in "giving him the space he needs when the angry pattern begins to escalate." The clinging found in anxious attachment and the ability to provide space are incompatible processes. Before any such "space giving" can occur, the woman will need help rebuilding her damaged self and separating it from the pattern of abuse. This missing therapeutic step indicates that Lawson has failed to take into account the victim's diminished or destroyed sense of self. Second, there is no need for a therapist to avoid forming a coalition with the emotionally abused woman. She is a victim and in need of validation and affirmation. Providing these reassurances does not preclude empathizing with the abuser, suggesting ways for him to deal with his anger, and supporting his appropriate caring and warm behaviors toward his partner.

Third, the abusive behavior *is* monstrous, and this reality should be pointed out to both victim and abuser in an objective and supportive manner. The therapist should label his behavior as emotional abuse and validate the victim's feelings and perceptions. By requesting that he stop it, the therapist makes reducing violence an important goal of therapy. The shared acknowledgment of his emotional abuse allows the woman to begin disattaching from the pattern of abuse; her reaction may be one of relief and welcome of the therapist's support and advocacy. By recognizing the abuse she will gain a new tool for empowering her efforts at self-protection. The abuser will gain, too, by learning to recognize his abuse and to increase his affectionate and supportive behavior. (The therapist's supportive role to both spouses is described more fully in Chapter 6.)

Fourth, it is unthinkable to blame the victim for violence committed against her. The emotionally abused woman is in no way responsible for the escalation of the violence, as is suggested by the systems perspective. Her anxious attachment and clinging behavior are responses to abuse, but they are no more instrumental in the escalation of violence than her adequacy, "overadequacy," submissiveness, or any other behavior.

Regardless of the victim's behavior, the emotional violence will escalate unless certain components of therapy are present. Chief among them is the abuser's acknowledgment that he is responsible for his violence. It must be clear that any changes in the victim's behavior the therapist suggests are *not* because she is in any sense a cause of the violence. This is true even when certain alterations in her actions are necessitated by the abuser's limited ability or unwillingness to change his behavior.

Lawson (1989) acknowledges that the systems approach to battering is "still in the beginning stages" (p. 373) and that few treatment conceptualizations and approaches are available for couples therapy when abuse is present. While theories abound, they are supported by little in the way of actual therapeutic techniques.

Relational Theory

As the above discussion makes clear, there has been a lack of research and therapeutic focus on women who are emotionally abused but not physically battered. Often the therapeutic perspectives and techniques developed for physically battered women are not as effective for women experiencing primarily or solely emotional abuse. An exception to this generalization is relational theory.

Most theoretical systems view interaction as unidirectional. Depression, for example, is often described in terms of one person's reaction to the loss of a partner. Relational theory, however, recognizes not only the disappointment and loss but also the two-way nature of the relational process:

> As our theory stresses, psychological development, especially for girls, is based on mutual understandings and reciprocity of affect. It is the flow of empathic communication and mutual attentiveness from one to the other that not only permits the child to feel cared for but begins to develop in the child a sense of herself as a caring being, as one who derives strength and competence from her own relational capacities. (Kaplan, 1991, p. 217)

Relational theory contends that women have traditionally built their sense of identity and self-worth on activities that involve caring about and giving to others. Being producers and caretakers of people, however, has not been considered a valuable activity in our culture. Because their strengths have not been defined as valid, worthwhile, or even as real activities, many women grow up with "a pervasive sense that what they do does not matter as much as what men do" (J. B. Miller, 1986, p. 76). They may be unable to "value and credit their own thoughts, feelings, and actions. It is as if they have lost a full sense of satisfaction in the use of themselves and all of their own resources—or rather, never had the full right to do so in the first place." (p. 90).

Describing society's tendency to discount women's qualities and negate their traditional accomplishments illuminates the vulnerability that is such an important feature of emotional abuse. Even before the abuse begins, the foundation has been laid by earlier experiences that predispose many women to internalize the culture's devaluation of their self, leading them to tolerate the discounting and negation characteristic of emotionally abusive relationships; they simply fail to recognize these as abuse and assume that such treatment is deserved. Social groups treated this way by the dominant society may exhibit a similar susceptibility to abuse.

Relational theory also helps clarify the role of empathy in relationships and the fear of abandonment that is so evident in the accounts of emotionally abused women, who value the rare moments of connection with the abuser and suffer profound loneliness and "empathy hunger" when it is withdrawn. The diminution of the self that occurs during emotional abuse leaves them with nothing to fall back on when the abuser threatens to leave.

Other explanations offered by relational theory are relevant to the emotionally abused woman's fear of abandonment. Women in general, according to Miller (1986), are hesitant to develop and become fully themselves. Being authentic means acknowledging and expressing anger and pursuing one's own interests and needs; it opens up the possibility of displeasing others. This in turn arouses fears of abandonment by the important other, "the person in whom her major emotional attachment is invested. If it is the male partner, her whole economic livelihood and social status are usually involved as well" (p. 110). This anticipation of incurring another's displeasure deters many women from expressing their ideas or challenging the dominant way of defining reality:

> As soon as many women think of incurring someone else's displeasure—especially a man's—they equate it with abandonment. The risk, in its psychic meaning and impact, becomes the risk of abandonment and condemnation. (The woman will be left because she was wrong and bad.) (p. 110)

Relational theory also sheds light on other components of emotional abuse. It has been suggested, for example, that because of the way in which women are socialized, many have not had the opportunity to define themselves: "Women come from a position in which their own nature was defined for them by others. Their selves were almost totally determined by what the dominant culture believed it needed from women and therefore induced women to try to be" (Miller, 1986, p. 118). Applied to emotional abuse, this point offers an insight into how women learn to submit to others' self-definitions—one of the classic dynamics found in emotional abuse. The historical and current experience of other groups vulnerable to being defined by the dominant society may also be explained by this theory.

The therapeutic goals of therapists who espouse relational theory therefore place great emphasis on helping the woman to discover and define herself. The therapist and client explore ways in which connections are structured by social and family expectations so that the client may develop and pursue her own values and style of connecting.

In the view of Carol Gilligan (1982), many women follow the message of the dominant culture to engage in a "denial of self" that precludes the search "for the truth of their own experience" (p. 145). They have accepted the perspective presented to them as the only legitimate worldview. One therapeutic response to this situation is offering support for a paradigm shift. For example, a woman who had accepted her father's ethic that one must always succeed came to question his dictum; she discovered that there were things more important to her than total success (pp. 145–156). This involved a paradigm shift away from a perspective that had been an "anchor of her identity and a bond between her father and herself" (p. 145). Able now to define her own reality and recognize the legitimacy of different worldviews, she felt more embedded in her self and appreciated both the differences and the connections between people.

According to relational theory, the woman's self develops in the context of these connections, in the "experience of emotional and cognitive inter-subjectivity: the ongoing, intrinsic inner awareness and responsiveness to the continuous existence of the other or others and the expectation of mutuality in this regard" (Surrey, 1991a, p. 61). Within relationships they find empathy and interdependence,

> a way of being in the world as part of a unit larger than the individual, where the "whole" is experienced as greater than the sum of the parts. The relationship or the new relational unit (e.g., couple, family, friendship, network, or work groups) comes to have a unique existence beyond the individuals, to be attended to, cared about, and nurtured. In this model the self gains vitality and enhancement in relationship and is not reduced or threatened by connections. (p. 62)

Relational theory also suggests that "the fundamental processes of mutual relationship are mutual engagement (attention and interest), mutual *empathy*, and mutual *empowerment*" (Surrey, 1991b, p. 167; italics in original).

An ultimate goal of growth, therefore, is to develop mutually empathic and empowering relationships. In such relationships, individuals are empowered by seeing and responding to each other;

engaging in interaction makes them more aware both of themselves and of each other. Even in the physical absence of the other, the "capacity to act in relationship" enables those who have developed it to realize and take into consideration the other's needs (p. 167).

Thus an important goal of the relational therapist who works with an emotionally abused woman is to help her experience empowerment by learning about new ways to connect, empathize, and respond in relationships. As she develops methods to disattach from the pattern of abuse, the survivor can begin to develop genuinely empathic and emotionally safe connections. The reintegration of the self can then take place in relationship to new, nonabusive connections with others and within a community.

Relational theory's focus on mutuality also offers insights into the behavior of certain emotional abusers. Jordan (1991) points out that imbalances in mutuality "if they occur in primary relationships . . . create significant pain [and] . . . boundary rigidity (discomfort with self-disclosure and difficulty allowing another to have an emotional impact)." The resultant impediment to mutuality causes one partner to be "walled off, inaccessible, or disconnected" (p. 90). An abused woman often feels that her partner is emotionally absent; he does not talk about his deep hopes or fears or help create an environment of mutual trust.

Abused children who later become abusers often adopt this walled-off posture as a way of dealing with pain. Later, their emotional inaccessibility to a partner renders them unable to connect with empathy or to consider another's needs. Their world-view encompasses only their own wishes, ideas, and feelings, which they often project onto the partner. In this narcissistic perspective, the abuser displays an egocentric focus; he "uses others to shore up his self-esteem. . . . The other does not exist as a whole person about whom he feels concerned and caring" (Jordan, 1991, p. 91).

The value of relational theory as a perspective for exploring emotional abuse is that it captures the full picture of the individual, those with whom she is connecting, and the larger social context. Instead of focusing on pathological interpretations of human behavior, it builds on a model of health and development. It views barriers to mutual empathy and empowerment as problematic.

The relevance of this perspective to emotional abuse is clear. The victim, struggling to develop in relation to her partner, meets only occasional warmth and understanding that is constantly interrupted by discounts and negation of her sense of self. This results in multiple disconnections and her fervent wish for a greater degree and consistency of empathy and validation. Emotional abuse victims report how much they value, and even cherish, the infrequent moments of empathic connection they share with the partner. Even though the mechanisms of abuse preclude genuine, ongoing mutual empathy, victims of emotional abuse persist in their attempts to connect with the partner. Every day they wrestle with the self-doubt and internalized self-criticism caused by current and past abuse. They often feel inadequate, unworthy, and self-destructive. Fearing to share their feelings and ideas—since this often brings on more abuse and threats of abandonment—they remain isolated and profoundly lonely.

The Attachment–Trauma Model of Emotional Abuse

An effective model of therapy for emotional abuse victims must include relational theory's emphasis on the self in connection with others. The hope for these victims lies in a therapeutic intervention that helps them develop new strategies and strengths in relating to important others and significant institutions. Based on the attachment–trauma model of emotional abuse presented in Chapters 1 through 4, this theoretical perspective of emotional abuse views the victim's symptomatology as a reaction to the abuse process. The therapeutic approach based on this perspective is described in depth in Chapter 6.

6

A New Model of Therapy

Working with emotionally abused clients is a challenge for therapists and advocates. These clients present with intrusive thoughts and images, profound sadness, and occasional somatic problems. Painful memories and a deep sense of isolation may interfere with concentration and make it difficult for them to hear and retain the therapist's observations and interpretations. The abuse process has eroded their sense of self and fundamentally affected their ability to connect with others.

Unaware of the abuse process, the client often blames herself for the problems. She may intersperse complaints about the relationship with expressions of love and tenderness for the abuser. Her keen sensitivity and empathic abilities help her to sense that his rage, cruelty, and intermittent warmth are reflections of his own fears and past experiences. In many cases this ambivalence is a pervasive obstacle to recognizing that she has been emotionally abused.

There are four important components in working with emotionally abused clients:

- Therapeutic stance
- Therapeutic endeavor
- Therapeutic modality
- Transformation

Therapeutic stance refers to the philosophical and ethical position therapists need to establish with their clients. I discuss this component in detail later in the chapter. The *therapeutic endeavor* component or phase involves helping the client recognize and acknowledge all aspects of emotional abuse. *Therapeutic modality* includes three subcomponents essential to the treatment of emotional abuse: validation, disattachment, and reintegration. Finally, *transformation* from victim to survivor is the crucial goal of treatment.

The therapeutic model for emotional abuse described in this chapter is based on the treatment and study of 376 heterosexual women at the Center for Mental Health and Human Development in Atlanta. It has also been used to help 7 heterosexual men, 39 children, 8 adolescents, 59 older adults, 13 lesbians, 16 gay men, and 11 prostitutes (female). The center specializes in the prevention and treatment of emotional and physical abuse. The Emotional Abuse Institute, a part of the center, serves as a "think tank" for the development of theories, training modules, and intervention strategies in the area of emotional abuse.

The effectiveness of this model has been measured by self-reports of clients, reports of partners, observations by the therapist, and a review of the case records by two independent therapists. The latter's judgments were based on criteria selected to reflect not only a decrease in symptoms, but also enhanced quality of life. The criteria included decrease of such symptoms as suicidal ideation, depression, sleep disturbances, automobile accidents, confusion, difficulty in concentration, nightmares, painful memories, intrusive thoughts, flashbacks, and feelings of despair. Other criteria were progress toward an integrated sense of self, a capacity to separate from the abusive process, involvement in activities that enhance self-satisfaction and self-confidence, quality contacts (connections) with family/ friends, and enthusiasm for life. There was general agreement between the two reviewing therapists. Moreover, the reviewers' evaluations of individual clients' progress were consistent with the reports of the clients themselves at termination of treatment.

The reviews indicated that following utilization of the therapeutic modality, all the women, men, and children in the study seemed to experience a decrease—in varying degrees—in disturbing symptoms. All clients appeared to exhibit some gains in the enjoyment of life and the ability to separate themselves from the abuse process. Intrusive thoughts, flashbacks, painful memories, and nightmares decreased or stopped.

When occasional such intrusive images as flashbacks and intrusive thoughts recurred during periods of intense stress, clients reported heightened confidence in their ability to cope with them. They also reported feeling a stronger sense of self, accompanied by a lessening of confusion, depression, and profound sadness. More frequent empathic interactions with family, friends, and others in social and recreational groups resulted in decreased feelings of loneliness.

Furthermore, in follow-up telephone interviews conducted (by prior arrangement) six and twelve months after the end of treatment, clients reported that therapeutic goals had been maintained. Most (75 percent) were not currently in therapy. Of the 25 percent who reentered therapy within a year of termination, most had returned to the therapist they had worked with prior to the study. During treatment with the new model, these clients had expressed a wish to continue therapy with the former therapist, whom they "trusted" and believed "really cares about me." Milly, a twenty three-year-old student, described the return to her former therapist as a valuable one:

> I really like my therapist. She didn't seem to understand how lost I really was, that I needed help with understanding and combatting the emotional abuse. But I am really happy to get back to her and be able to work with her again. Now I can hear her ideas better, and I can sleep well and concentrate.

Among the larger group who perceived themselves as able to maintain the therapeutic goals when not in therapy, most (1) called the therapist and engaged in one to four telephone conversations and/or (2) requested up to three interviews during the year after termination. At the end of treatment with the emotional abuse model, I made a contract with clients, giving them the right to utilize me as a consultant. Both the telephone calls and the interviews that resulted from this contract were occasional, short-term, and characterized by the client's ability to reintegrate treatment goals during a crisis.

Therapeutic Stance

In the context of emotional abuse, *therapeutic stance* refers to respect for the client's unfolding self. Learning about the client's hobbies, interests, and buried dreams and hopes is an essential aspect of the therapeutic stance. Expressions of interest and enthusiasm for her talents or skills represent the sort of positive regard and belief in her abilities that have long been missing from her life. If she has experienced emotional abuse in her current and past relationships, she may never have enjoyed this kind of validation.

Together, the therapist and client search for the golden nuggets of ability and interest hidden amid the murky symptoms of abuse. This is the survivor's quest for hope. The therapist is, in part, a coach who helps guide and teach the client while applauding the development of her skills. Whether the talent is for writing, photography, sports, dancing, science, or career development, the warm and empathic connection formed between client and therapist during this quest becomes a model for the client's subsequent connections. Although marked by mutual self-disclosure, the focus is always on the client's growth, pain, fears, hopes, and eventual empowerment. Some therapists prefer to locate areas of the client's interest and refer them elsewhere for exploration, while other therapists conduct in-depth examinations and planning with the client for development of skills, interests, and dreams.

Betty was a forty-six-year-old former social worker married to a wealthy and successful lawyer. He had insisted that Betty give up her job while their four children were growing up. Caught in an emotionally abusive relationship, Betty had become depressed and confused; she experienced intrusive thoughts and minor flashbacks. Betty was hospitalized briefly after admitting that she had suicidal thoughts. She had been in therapy—primarily joint counseling sessions with her husband—for a year. When Betty asked if she could terminate therapy because her depression was deepening, the therapist referred her to the center for treatment. Later, at the end of her treatment with the new therapy model, Betty discussed the insidious nature of emotional abuse and the importance of the therapeutic stance:

> My husband is so handsome and smooth that no one recognized his
> continual, subtle undercutting of me. I, myself, never really saw the be-

littling and control for what it was. I lost myself and my ability to analyze. Anyway, this four months of therapy that has focused on emotional abuse was like a trip with a camping partner. You [the therapist]
explored every mechanism of his abuse with me. In fact, there were
two consulting interviews where you confronted him about specific
put-downs. I had an advocate who was so "for me" that she didn't rest
until I told her my hidden dream of getting a doctorate in psychology.
And now I have been accepted in a doctoral program!

In the therapeutic stance, the therapist not only helps uncover
and develop the client's hopes and dreams, he or she validates the
client's feelings, ideas, and perceptions. The emotionally abused
client, a prey to frequent despair and anguish, desperately needs to
feel valued and comforted in order to experience hope again. The
therapist and client must therefore explore creative strategies to
help her find ways to comfort herself rather than turn to drugs, al-
cohol, or eating disorders.

The specific manner in which therapists comfort their clients will
depend on their own style and the specific needs of the client.
There are, however, certain underlying needs shared by all who
have experienced emotional abuse. For the despairing and emotionally isolated person, the therapist's "being there" may be a new
experience, knowing "for the first time in his life what it means to
have someone on his side, an advocate" (Sakheim & Devine, 1992,
p. 285).

Thus, on both conscious and unconscious levels, the client is experiencing "reconnective integrated interaction." Connection with
the therapist is marked by an empathic and supportive presence
while the survivor's fragmented and diminished sense of self becomes more integrated in this connection.

Victims describing painful incidents of emotional abuse and reliving them as major or minor flashbacks experience an *abreaction*;
that is, they recall and reexperience both recent and long-term
abuse simultaneously. To "risk remembering" (p. 286), they must
feel that they are in a partnership of emotional safety, comfort, and
hope. Physical contact between therapist and client may help ce-
ment such a partnership.

Patients going through an abreaction can be helped tremendously by
such contact and will often report feeling less alone, more supported,

more connected to the safety of the present, less . . . untouchable. (pp. 285–286)

There are numerous *nonsexual* physical gestures by which the therapist can "be there" for the disconnected and despairing victim. He or she may hug a client or hold her hand (p. 286), or rest a hand momentarily on a victim's shoulder. Placing a hand under a client's elbow and holding it there for a few moments is a symbolic gesture of support.

Prior to any physical touching of a client, however, two therapeutic steps must be performed. First, the therapist should *ask* the client about her wishes in a particular instance. Would she like a hug, feel comforted by an arm around the shoulder when she is weeping, or find a pat on the shoulder soothing? *Some clients do not wish to be touched.* Second, at the outset of any therapy with an emotionally abused individual—adult or child—the therapist needs to convey to the client that *no exploitation will occur.* If the therapist receives permission to hug an adult client, male or female, the client needs to know that *sexual expression between client and therapist is not acceptable.* All physical contact should be presented as gestures of caring, protection, and respect. Thereafter, any question regarding whether a hug would be comforting is placed in the context of what *feels safe to the client* and is based on the initial *nonsexual contract.*

Of course, therapists need to be sensitive and self-protective as well. One male therapist confided to me that he sees no female clients after five o'clock, when his colleagues leave the office. Furthermore, he leaves his door open slightly when evaluating female clients for the first time—to reassure them of his nonexploitative intent and "to protect myself against false accusations until I know and trust a client." It is best to exercise this sort of caution with clients of both sexes.

Even though the therapeutic stance makes the therapist an advocate of the emotionally abused client, it does not imply that he or she is the enemy of the woman's partner. Rather, the abusive individual should be viewed as an ally and as a person who also needs support, clarification, and therapeutic coaching. He should be asked to attend therapy sessions once in a while (two or three times only) as a consultant (1) to help ascertain the kind of abuse a client is facing, (2) to alter that abuse, and (3) to participate in the process of encouraging and supporting the client's growth.

Valerie was a fifty-three-year-old factory worker whose husband of thirty-three years, Jeff, emotionally abused her with jealousy, isolation, put-downs, and negative labeling. While acting supportively toward Valerie, the therapist also attempted to support Jeff. Initially, however, Jeff refused to come to the therapist's office. In a case like this, when the abuser is resistant to treatment, the therapist can telephone the abusive person to encourage participation. Or, considering safety and the style of the therapist, some therapists may choose to make a home visit if the abusive person expresses his willingness. During a home visit, his views of what is important in life become evident. Valerie described what happened when her therapist visited their home:

> If I'm not home from work at the factory right on the dot, he's mad and jealous. He didn't want to come into therapy—thought he'd get yelled at or something, I guess. Then you [therapist] came out to see him and talked to him about his baseball cards. He thought you were OK. Then he came into therapy, and you told him to stop interrupting me and saying my ideas were silly when he did it in front of you. You said he should treat me as good as his baseball cards. He was amazed [and] said he didn't know he'd been mean, but you said right to him, "Yeah, pretty mean all right." And you said he could do better and could help you and me, and he puffed up and felt proud.

In therapy Valerie revealed that she had always dreamed of returning to college and finishing the degree she had abandoned prior to marrying. Her husband attended an interview to discuss her dream and what role he could play in its actualization. In the subsequent therapy session, Valerie discussed the joint interview, in which he had been treated as a consultant while she made her own decisions about her life:

> You asked him how he'd help, and he said he'd buy my schoolbooks. You asked me if that was OK. I felt like my own boss. You warned him he'd get jealous, and you asked me if I'd leave him and I said, "Naw, I want him." He cried and said he was scared of that. He did buy my books, and I am in school. I still get scared when he gets jealous. If I say, "Remember what my therapist said?" he calms down quicker. He

never hit me, but like you said, his words hurt like a fist. So now I want to feel more sure, 'cause I still wonder if I did something wrong when he gets jealous.

The therapist of an emotionally abused woman should be realistic about the kind and amount of change that an abuser will make. Many have a limited willingness and/or ability to change their behavior and seldom follow up on a recommendation to seek therapy for work on their own issues. Most of the time, the therapist will need to make a special effort to connect, by telephone or in person, and to convince the abuser to attend an individual session and to take part in a subsequent consulting session(s).

During such consultancy sessions, the abuser is permitted to offer ideas and express his feelings but not to control or "own" his partner's growth. Over time he may be invited to a total of two or three consulting interviews. Before the first one, the therapist should meet with him individually to get acquainted and encourage him to share his vulnerable feelings and make specific requests of his partner. He can be coached in how to practice mutually empathic connections, how not to focus so much on himself that he fails to see what others are feeling, and how to drop his "walls" and allow his own feelings to show.

An abuser may participate fully in therapy if the therapist tells him it is important for his partner's well-being and if he is treated as a supportive ally. When the therapist views him as someone the victim loves, he will probably be willing to negotiate ways of becoming part of the comforting, encouraging team.

Although few emotionally abusive men recognize the full import of their violence, most are willing to make some changes to assist the therapeutic process. A small percentage of emotionally abusive individuals are so sadistic and cruel, however, that no changes are possible. They are too heavily invested in continuing the violence. This will become evident early in therapy as they fail to decrease their emotional assaults over time. In these cases, the therapist needs to acknowledge the situation to the victim. Years later some clients have reported, like Nancy, that the acknowledgment was itself a springboard for subsequent change:

I'm calling you [the therapist] to let you know about a big change I've made in my life. I heard what you said to me in therapy six years ago, even though you might not have thought so. At that time I seemed pretty stuck to staying with Howard. But last year we were divorced—at my request. I began to see the cruelty in his behavior, like you said. When I let him know how unhappy I was, he agreed to a divorce.

Therapeutic Endeavor

While establishing the therapeutic stance, the therapist develops the therapeutic endeavor. This consists of (1) an empathic connection with the therapist, (2) enhanced recognition and clarification about important abuse components, and (3) a process of working through trauma. The client-therapist connection—characterized by honesty and validation—serves as the initial pathway to restoration of the diminished or destroyed self. Together, therapist and client explore and learn to recognize those components of the self disrupted by the abusive process and "the powers which threatened to rob you of your very self" (Frankl, 1963, p. 104).

This reconnective integrated interaction is both the vehicle for restoration of the self and the model for empathic connection. Initially the victim may have great difficulty envisioning a more consistently mutual empathic connection. If she has a long history of emotional abuse, her current situation may seem normal to her. Like Anne Sexton's victim, she knows no alternative to emotional captivity:

fastened to the wall like a bathroom plunger,
held like a prisoner
who was so poor
he fell in love with jail. (Sexton, 1966, p. 10)

During the therapeutic endeavor, the therapist helps the victim recognize the effects and components of emotional abuse: The diminished sense of self, attachment anxiety, overt and covert levels of abuse, mechanisms of abuse, the possible presence of physical and/or sexual abuse, emotional trauma, and the hunger for connection. Throughout the process, the therapist utilizes a dual therapeutic approach: Continually recognizing these components and clarifying the way they operate on the victim's self, while consistently validating the client's own perceptions and feelings about the abusive relationship. Recognizing the components of emotional abuse is crucial to providing the client with clarification about the abuse process and its effects on her. Failure to do so can lead to misdiagnosis, use of inappropriate therapeutic techniques, unnecessary hospitalization, and the client's inability to thrive and grow.

One method of clarification some therapists and clients feel comfortable with is the Emotional Abuse Climate Map (see Figure 2). The therapist develops this map—which is a little like a weather chart—in partnership with the client. Together they list each type of abuse manifested in the relationship (discounting, negation, denial, projection, negative labeling, abandonment, threats, and so forth) and inscribe each one in a circle in the left-hand vertical column. Drawing an arrow from each circle to the middle column, they describe in a few words specifically how the abuse is manifested. (In Figure 2, for example, the arrow from the circle labeled "threats" leads to the middle column, which lists "to leave me.") Lastly, they draw another arrow leading to the third (far right) column and fill in the victim's primary reactions to the abuse. A few additional words can be added to clarify further how a reaction is manifested. "Fear," for example, might describe the primary feeling aroused by the threat to abandon, while "nightmares" underneath it could specify the way the fear is manifested. Another section of the map might start with the words "put-downs" or "discount/negative labeling" in the left-hand circle. Here the middle column might include "interrupts me," "uses disgusted tone of voice," and "calls me dumb and boring," while the far right column lists words reflecting the victim's feelings, such as "sadness," "confusion," and "loneliness."

When complete, the map describes the emotional climate in which the client lives. This helps her to conceptualize the abuse process and its impact on her. It can become a springboard for discussing the client's anxious attachment to the abuser. How do the feelings evoked by the abuse translate into clinging behavior during her desperate attempts to gain validation and warmth from him? Does the behavior intensify her loneliness and yearning for a more mutual connection? Does it result in a decrease of her self-esteem? One victim looking at this dynamic for the first time reported feeling "demeaned by having to beg for warmth and feeling such abject degradation."

Figure 2.
Emotional Abuse Climate Map

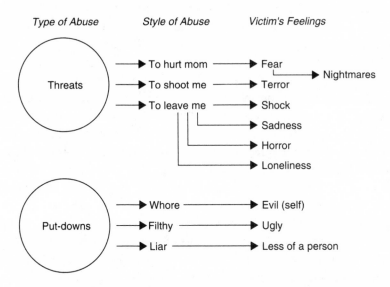

This tool can also facilitate the diagnosis of emotional abuse and the therapist's assessment of its severity and mechanisms:

> The therapist must have a map to guide them [*sic*] in this difficult journey, with the hope and wisdom to coax the client out of the darkness and chaos of the violated inner world. The assessment and conceptualization serve as this guide, with the first area to negotiate being the self. (McCann & Pearlman, 1990b, p. 138)

The therapist's feedback about the client's responses in therapy is another mechanism of clarification. By commenting when the client seems uncertain and self-doubting, the therapist can help her see that the abuse has reduced or diminished some of her self. Many clients describe feeling "relief" and "hope" when offered labels for their emotions of confused loss and desperation. They feel less crazy and frightened when they learn that their symptoms are traumatic reactions to severe stress. It helps to understand the theoretical basis for the feelings and the fact that "many assaults . . . particularly repetitive assaults by family members, also produce a wider array of post-traumatic symptoms, including distorted patterns of attachment, pervasive problems of identity integration, and belief systems that rationalize assaultive behavior" (Waites, 1993, p. 86).

Emotional assaults can result in hearing or visual impairments in which severe trauma actually blocks out frightening sights or sounds. Mattie, the account discussed previously, reported having flashbacks in which she saw her father screaming at her when she was six years old but could hear no sound coming from his lips. Sometimes when her husband yelled at her the same thing happened, and she was terrified. In another case, a frightened client could see only a blur instead of the body of her husband coming toward her in a threatening manner: "I felt like I was going crazy and couldn't even see him." Understanding that such frightening experiences of impaired or distorted perception are normal reactions to emotional assault can be very reassuring.

Asking clarifying questions is a valuable way to open a discussion of possible abuse. The therapist can ask, "Do you experience any frightening symptoms?" or "Does your partner make critical and demeaning comments about your clothes or your personality?" Remember that it is a paradigm shift for a client to think of herself as traumatized and demeaned in her relationship instead of unattractive, worthless, crazy, or mean.

Rebuilding, rediscovering, and nurturing the client's self is an essential part of the therapeutic endeavor and the client-therapist connection. The therapist will help the client clarify for herself answers to such questions as "Who is my self?" and "What are the interests, enjoyments, vulnerabilities, talents, and aspirations of this person who is me?" A useful technique is to ask about times in the past when others have encouraged her to develop some treasured dream or complimented her on an accomplishment. Asking such directional questions can help her put the emotional abuse process in perspective and begin to diminish its destructive effects. Thus, through her connection with the therapist, the client's past strengths and present hopes can become signposts to guide the journey toward becoming a survivor.

It is also important for the therapist to facilitate the client's search for new directions and forging of new human connections. The therapist will help the survivor see that the self develops in three connections: (1) with its own growing awareness of itself as a separate and valuable entity; (2) with nonabusive and validating others who embrace the client's existence and marvel at her uniqueness; and (3) with ideals, causes, and institutions in the larger society that fit the client's growing sense of identity.

The survivor will need to develop compassion toward her existential pain and despair that stem from diminishment of both the self and the meaning in life. Sharing a recognition of her own anxious attachment with the therapist should lead to understanding of the painful basis of her clinging behaviors. She and the therapist must accept her internalized self-disgust, harshness, and self-criticism with understanding and gentle tolerance. Recalling and reexperiencing childhood and adult emotional abuse can add to her empathic self-understanding and help her find her new ways of connecting with her inner self and others. One client described the new understanding of her self gained in therapy this way:

> I've never known any other form of connection, so how can I keep beating myself up on account of having one after another painful attachments? Besides, why don't I try being as kind to myself as I wish my partner would be to me? You [therapist] are understanding and ask me to treat myself like I was my own guest at the Ritz Carlton Hotel. It's fun being gracious with myself. It's new and gentle. I'm more understanding with others now, too.

By providing the client with reassurances that her behaviors are understandable in the circumstances she faces, the therapist helps the survivor learn to reassure herself. She needs to hear that it is natural for anxiously attached individuals to grasp desperately at elusive moments of human warmth and affection. Such a perspective lets her know that there is no deficit in herself and that by clinging to the abuser she is having a normal reaction to traumatic circumstances.

Both therapist and client need to understand the depth of desperation an emotionally abused person experiences when threatened with emotional and/or physical abandonment. She perceives the attachment to the abuser as her lifeline to emotional survival; suffering from the diminished sense of self wrought by the abuse and isolated from other human contact, she is not mistaken. Her survival does depend on warmth and validation that can only come, currently, from him.

For this reason, it is not therapeutically feasible for the therapist at this stage to encourage the client to "detach" or leave the abuser. There is no self strong enough to detach. Decisions about various levels of possible disattachment can be made when the anxious attachment has lessened and the client herself decides it is appropriate to do so. Therefore, *in the absence of life-threatening physical abuse*, any decision regarding separation or divorce should be delayed until therapy has progressed further. In the meantime, the therapist should reassure the client that she will become skilled in self-caring and will recognize when the time has come to consider these steps. In fact, many survivors report feeling relieved of the pressure of making any immediate decision and enjoy the feeling of being trusted to resolve this issue at the right time. *Neither staying in the relationship nor this entire mode of therapy is appropriate when physically battered women are experiencing life-threatening abuse.* Such victims require a different category of treatment, which I will address later in this chapter.

Another important aspect of the therapeutic endeavor is the Connection–deprivation Cycle (see Figure 3). Most clients are aware of their partner's swings in and out of connection but do not necessarily recognize the role the swings play in their own clinging behavior. When the abuser allows a brief period of connection after evoking his partner's terrified anxiety through discounts and threats, it is to satisfy his own needs or to manipulate and control her. To begin gaining some control over this process herself, therefore, the client must become aware of her responses in the context of this cycle of connection–disconnection–trauma–anxious clinging–continued abuse–intermittent warmth–connection.

This crucial endeavor involves (1) identifying the style of the survivor's clinging; (2) empowering her to halt it; and (3) offering her alternative models of connecting. It also includes clarifying for the survivor the process of "coming apart"—or disintegration—and encouraging her developing skill at reintegrating the self.

Exploration, clarification, reassurance, and encouragement of the cycle should begin early in the therapeutic endeavor. Together, therapist and client will identify the various forms of clinging, including attempts to keep the abuser from leaving the house, insistence on continued conversation when he is unresponsive, requests for hugs or other displays of affection, and attempts to obtain verbal reassurance and/or validation from the resistant abuser. The

Figure 3.
The Connection–deprivation Cycle

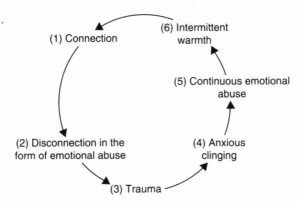

therapist will help the client recognize the unfolding tragedy as the abuser responds to her struggle for connection with additional verbal abuse, withdrawal, rejection, and denigration.

The therapist can provide hope and reassurance that the struggle will eventually have a different outcome. He or she should warn the client that in the meantime confusion, depression, and trauma may result from it. Some victims strike out at the abuser or harm themselves by self-mutilation, substance abuse, or attempting suicide. The therapist needs to discuss these risks with the client.

Another important aspect of the therapeutic endeavor is the clarification and normalization of somatic symptoms that frequently result from traumatic emotional abuse. Gwen was a seventy-two-year-old retired banker whose husband Eddie had been emotionally abusive for the entire fifty years of their marriage. She presented for therapy with chest pains, headaches, and stomachaches for which no medical basis could be found. She sensed that her own desperate clinging behavior and resulting low self-esteem was affecting her physically:

> I've been retired for two years and have felt sick most of the time. Sometimes I get aches in my head and chest. When Eddie is unhappy, he threatens to leave me and I feel terrific chest pains, like my heart is bursting. He calls me worthless and says he wishes I was dead. I feel so desperate trying to get him to say he loves me while he kind of smirks and says not a word. How have I dropped from being a bank officer to this begging, demeaning posture?

The therapist assured Gwen that her behavior and physical pain were normal reactions to emotional abuse. When this therapist interpreted the metaphor of a "bursting" heart as an emotional response to Eddie's abuse, Gwen's "heartaches" stopped. She began to be more gentle with herself once she understood "why I'm different with him than I was when I was a respected bank officer."

A client may experience forms of emotional and/or physical behavior she does not perceive as abusive, even though they are violent and intimidating. If the therapist does not ask about them directly, the client may not initially report such actions as threats, shoving her, holding her down against her will, throwing items, grabbing or twisting her arms and legs, slamming doors or furniture, and pet abuse.

It is important for both therapist and client to recognize that emotional abuse creates barriers to concentration, feelings of confusion, shock, nightmares, painful memories, intrusive thoughts, and flashbacks. The therapist needs to ask about such symptoms openly and directly ("Do you have images or thoughts that persist in your mind for long periods of time?" "When you are describing that abusive incident, does it seem as if it is happening all over again?" "How real is that experience for you right now?").

Mildred, who had left college to get married and reentered college years later, experienced difficulty concentrating on her schoolwork and sought counseling. For years her husband had emotionally abused her in a number of ways, including isolating her from family and friends. In therapy, Mildred recognized that her emotional wounds were responsible for her difficulties:

> I just can't think about my assignments, because I keep thinking about Rollie and what he says about me—that I'm selfish and mean to spend time on schoolwork. He says I am so dumb that I won't do well anyway, and I'm scared he's right. After we get into arguments, I keep thinking about what he said and what I said, and the thoughts dance around in my mind. I need to study for a test, but instead I worry about whether to wear this blouse, which Rollie says is too tempting to other men.

Mildred learned to recognize these intrusive thoughts and the abusive mechanisms that caused them. Understanding how the emotional violence affected her allowed Mildred to grieve over the repeated loss of warmth, feel the pain of her inner wounds, and de-crease the intrusive thinking. With the help of the therapist she was able to focus and concentrate better.

The therapist also focused on Mildred's minor flashbacks. Using relaxation exercises, Mildred was able to experience flashbacks that involved reliving emotional abuse from both her childhood and her current relationship. Mildred described feelings of profound loneli-ness and sadness, a sense of terror following her father's rageful screaming and negative labeling, and wishes to kill herself stem-ming back to her childhood. While this retrospective flashback re-call was very painful for Mildred, she reported that reliving these traumatic experiences during flashbacks enabled her to decrease the repetitive attempts to replay childhood scenes with Rollie while—during these trauma reenactments—she would desperately yearn for a different ending.

> But the endings were always the same. I'd reach out for affirmation of who I was and get crushed, over and over. I couldn't seem to stop the hope, and the repeated attempts to get my father and then Rollie, to say they thought I had a good idea in my head. And I never stopped being shocked at their rage.

Therapeutic Modality

The therapeutic stance, therapeutic endeavor, and therapeutic modality components of the emotional abuse model are utilized si-multaneously. Theresa experienced this blending of therapeutic ele-ments:

> Sometimes I feel like I am on a train journey with you [therapist] trav-eling along. You point out the important sites or abusive processes, while I begin to feel desperate and have intrusive thoughts. Then you help me escape from that mode and understand how to make meaning of it, all the time reminding me to pursue my journalistic writing for the newspaper. It's really no longer just a hobby, since they're printing my first article. I feel more like my self is coming back, and now I'm using the techniques to escape the abuse. Little by little, I'm not coming apart much anymore. Experiencing the flashbacks in therapy is scary at the time, but after I feel a sense of difference and peace.

The techniques described by Theresa reflect a threefold therapeutic intervention consisting of validation, disattachment, and reintegration.

Validation

In the validation process the therapist affirms the existence and worth of the client's self—her thoughts, ideas, perceptions, feelings, goals, and styles of behaving. Sometimes for many years these components of the self have been consistently discounted, negated, and negatively labeled.

During a consulting or joint interview the therapist should confirm, through discussion or observation, each abusive mechanism uncovered in individual sessions. Thus the validation process also serves as affirmation of the emotional abuse process itself. Validation that involves pointing out specific abuse observed in a relationship differs from the more general recognition and clarification that occur during the ongoing therapeutic endeavor.

In a consultancy session, the therapist may share a general recognition of an abusive mechanism with both parties—for example, by describing how put-downs and negative labels diminish the victim's sense of self. In a more focused validation the therapist would point to specific and repetitive instances or patterns of abuse. For example, he or she might comment to the abuser (in the presence of the victim), "Jeff, you often interrupt Jan and sound disgusted after she has expressed an idea, which you call 'stupid.'" Or the therapist may point out a specific comment and label it as emotional abuse: "Jeff, when you interrupt Jan, call her ideas 'silly' and say her plan is 'disgusting,' you are being emotionally abusive. I'd like for you to stop doing that."

Prior to the consulting sessions the therapist should meet with the abuser in an individual interview to allow for development of rapport. A meeting can also help the therapist learn about hobbies, business interests, values, fears, and life goals that may serve as useful contexts for framing confrontations. During the consulting sessions the therapist will point out instances of abusive behavior and suggest alternative, more empathic styles of connection:

Jeff, you keep criticizing Jan's ideas. I want to hear what Jan has to say, because she has good ideas. Do you think she has good ideas? Since you nod yes, then—as her partner—will you please tell her so and support her ideas the way you would when closing a good business deal? You're a successful businessman, and just as your company depends on your charm and negotiations, your support and caring are very important to Jan. If you're frightened of losing her when she goes to back to school, as you've said before, please just say that and give her a chance to reassure you.

A therapist who identifies emotional abuse during an initial joint interview should take it as an indication of the need for subsequent individual interviews with the victim. Because the therapist's first goal is to connect with and become an advocate for the abused woman, the therapeutic stance and endeavor should be developed prior to validating the client in the presence of the abuser's put-downs. At least three individual interviews with an emotionally abused client should precede a consulting interview.

Individual interviews with an abuser will provide the therapist with knowledge of his terms of reference and insights into his value system. As noted earlier, Valerie's therapist told Jeff, her husband, he should value his partner and treat her as gently as he did his treasured baseball cards; that is, he should brag about her worth to other people, just as he did with the cards. This comment precipitated a search in which he explored the qualities he most valued in his wife and figured out how he could communicate his appreciation to her.

Specific validations of a client's perceptions can sometimes be enhanced by developing an Emotional Abuse Climate Map, which was discussed earlier in relation to the clarification and recognition components of the therapeutic endeavor. While in practice there is an interweaving of the therapeutic endeavor and validation, it is valuable to distinguish between them. Moreover, a client is less able to hear and understand the therapist's specific validations until a foundation of more general recognition and clarification has been established in individual sessions.

Validation, which begins during therapy, is continued by the client herself. She learns to validate herself with compassion, enthusiasm, and self-support—whether in the presence of the therapist or on her own. Learning to validate oneself is a slow process for an individual whose self has been eroded, however, and the therapist will need to encourage her and celebrate self-validation (by a verbal congratulation, a small gift, or a card) when it occurs.

Julia was a psychologist who described "losing touch with the 'me' that is myself" when her woman partner criticized, demeaned, and humiliated her: "I thought being with a woman would allow an escape from abuse, but my lover is just as abusive as some men I know." Her therapist continued to provide validation until Julia became able to practice self-validation. She learned to hold encouraging internal conversations with herself:

> I say to myself, "Now look here; your idea is a good one, but she doesn't feel comfortable with it." She continues to put me down, even after you [therapist] told her in the consulting interview that it was emotional abuse to label someone "frivolous" and "dipsy" so often. The difference is that now I can say to her, "Here you go again with that put-down stuff." I feel angry, and yet I feel smart and competent, like you keep saying I am. So I tell myself that I really did well.

In therapy, validation techniques can be used to help a client cope with her reaction to emotional abuse, especially the confused feeling of "coming apart" described by so many emotionally abused individuals. Researchers have recognized the presence of this kind of cognitive disintegration, depression, and fear among victims of physical violence (Janoff-Bulman, 1988), as well as the tendency of trauma sufferers to experience a metaphorical death of the self (Niles, 1992a). The therapist's validation will both counteract the disintegration of the self—helping the victim see that she is responding normally to the trauma of emotional abuse—and encourage the growth of new skills like self-validation. When the therapist affirms that both the abuse process and the client's strengths and worth exist, confusion is eliminated. The abused woman's feeling of nonexistence (a primary trigger for disintegration and subsequent trauma) is transformed gradually into a cohesive sense of self. Sally experienced this crumbling of her self; she described feeling as if she were dead, a walking zombie. I was apart. During the abuse, I felt all broken up like Humpty Dumpty. I had car accidents. I was a mess. I felt like I was putting pieces of a puzzle back together when I started in therapy. Then you [therapist] would say, "No wonder you feel that way," and I felt more real and whole.

The therapist should validate intrusive thoughts and flashbacks as traumatic reactions to severe emotional abuse. Managing intrusive imagery involves exploring with the client the specific triggers to the nightmares, painful memories, intrusive thoughts, or flashbacks.

Do they tend to occur at night? While the student [client] is alone? Are they triggered by certain people who remind the student of the perpetrator, by television shows, climate. . . . Understanding the specific triggers to the emergence of memories is often a relief because these links are frequently unconscious. When they are made conscious, the student can begin to understand his or her responses in ways that enhance the experience of safety and control. (McCann & Pearlman, 1992, p. 194)

Identifying the triggers and validating the pain they evoke is valuable to a client, whose feelings have been discounted in the abuse process.

Nonetheless, therapists must be alert to the client's tolerance level for exploring and validating these triggers, examining them as a stronger self develops and asking periodically whether the material is too painful. Thus the therapist can simultaneously validate the client's feelings and give her permission to postpone the discussion to another session.

The therapist should also validate the client's need to stop the intrusive imagery when working or driving, helping her recognize warning signs and develop ways to ensure her safety—for example, by pulling the car into a *safe place* while experiencing intrusive images. The therapist can help work out emergency plans and warn her against driving immediately after an abusive incident, when intrusive imagery can detract from concentration. Additional techniques to achieve both emotional and physical safety must be explored in therapy.

This may include thinking through such questions as "Whom can I call? Where can I go for support? What do I need right now?" It is important to spend some time at the end of each session exploring with the survivor what he or she needs to calm and soothe himself or herself when distressed, how to mobilize resources when the memories are overwhelming, and so forth. . . . As a short term coping strategy, some people may find distraction useful—engaging in school activities, doing homework, or working crossword puzzles. (p. 194)

Unlike some other kinds of trauma, the assaults of emotional abuse are current and ongoing, not memories of past experiences. An important role for the therapist, therefore, is providing a model for day-to-day validating, comforting, and encouraging behavior. Developing the client's ability to soothe herself can help prevent self-destructive behaviors that stem from internalizing the abuser's criticism and disgust.

As the student survivor is increasingly able to cope with the painful, intrusive memories, she or he must eventually probe into and express the painful imagery in some detail. . . . The helper must be calm and soothing when the survivor is recalling an emotionally charged memory. . . . The helper might gently say, "Of course you feel sad; you were badly hurt." (p. 194)

When there are flashbacks or intrusive thoughts, validation can take the form of reminders that the client is becoming stronger, growing in therapy, working through traumatization, and improving her coping skills. Initially, however, these validating reminders will not dissipate the intrusive thoughts and flashbacks. They will persist for some time because the ongoing stress—the emotional abuse—does not fit into the client's scheme of thought. The client's deep conviction that it is not fair or logical to be emotionally assaulted by the person she loves and is attempting to please is denied by her daily experience. This dissonance is an impetus toward trauma and the resulting intrusive imagery.

When the client is still unaware of the emotional abuse process, this jarring may be only a vague feeling of unfairness. Or her complaint may center on one specific way in which she is mistreated. By validating the belief in the unfairness of the situation, the therapist helps the client let go of the struggle to render an emotionally abusive attachment either kind or fair—an impossible task.

A therapeutic modality that utilizes consultation, as well as transformation of the survivor through validation can help both partners move away from abuse and toward a more mutually respectful and empathic connection. The degree of movement the abuser can attain, however, varies a great deal from case to case. While limits can and should be set by the therapist and the client, there is no guarantee that the abuser will honor these limits and stop the emotional assaults. The therapist, therefore, needs to validate continually and realistically the client's inability to stop the assaults of either past or present abusive attachments—validating her real hopes for a transformation of the self that will make her less vulnerable to assault. A major component of this transformation will be her ability to disattach from the emotional abuse and its effects.

Disattachment

Disattachment is a twofold separation from the emotional abuse process and from the client's own traumatic reactions to it. It is part of the transformation of the self from a diminished and fragmented state to greater cohesion and integration. As I have emphasized at earlier points, it is unfair to expect disattachment early in therapy because of the ongoing abuse process, the client's desperation, and her diminished sense of self. As therapy progresses, however, the foundation of disattachment is laid in the client's increased ability to identify specific patterns of emotional abuse. As these components of abuse occur, the therapist describes options for disattaching from them. Movement away from the characteristic clinging responses to abuse, for example, can be encouraged by urging the client to develop self-nurturing, self-comforting, and self-validating behaviors. Hobbies or skills that are themselves self-validating can become alternatives to turning to the abuser for warmth and validation.

Working through, managing, and decreasing nightmares, painful memories, intrusive thoughts, and flashbacks is as important for the survivor as disattaching from the emotional abuse process. Otherwise, these relived aspects of the trauma will leave no emotional space for transformation, and the client will continue to be overwhelmed by them. McCann and Pearlman's work with college students experiencing traumatic recall of past abuse confirms the initial need to manage stress and back away from the intrusive imagery. Once this has been accomplished, client and therapist can examine the triggers and specific content of the intrusive imagery. This distancing of the imagery is crucial to avoiding retraumatization and embracing the process of disattachment.

> It is very important to explore techniques for backing away from painful memories before the memories become too overwhelming, otherwise some student survivors may retraumatize themselves. . . . Some techniques for assisting in backing away are taking planned "vacations" from the memory work . . . using imagery to move away temporarily from threatening material (e.g., one can go to one's "safe" place in one's mind through imagery), and developing ways of soothing and calming oneself through self-nurturing behaviors. (McCann & Pearlman, 1992, pp. 194–195).

Validating plans to provide emotional safety (like not driving when engaged in intrusive imagery) can be part of tolerating the painful thoughts and images for some period and waiting for them to end. But the process of disattachment also involves more active attempts to work through and halt these intrusive processes. Polly, a twenty-year-old student, had an emotionally abusive boyfriend who put her down by belittling her intelligence and insisting that she would fail her courses. She continually relived their discussions, hearing his voice calling her "dumb ass" and "she who would be better off dead." Whenever she was in the bathroom she experienced flashbacks of the sound of his steps coming to the door and demanding to be let in. If she asked him to wait, he took the door off the hinges. Even when he was not there she heard his mocking voice calling her ugly and stupid and saying she would be better off dead:

> During class last night, I kept thinking about what he said and feeling scared. I couldn't concentrate. I tried rubbing my finger on my wrist to calm down and it helped, like we practiced in the last therapy session. When you [therapist] asked me to do something that comforted me, it took me a long time to figure out rubbing my wrist because I'm not used to comforting myself. Your suggestion to imagine a white light cir-

cling and protecting me made me feel safer. And I tried hugging myself. At first it felt strange and then I felt calm, like a mother comforting a baby.

Developing the ability to disattach from the abusive process consistently is a complex assignment requiring the client to achieve a number of specific tasks: (1) adding self components not developed earlier in life, such as self-comforting skills and confidence in one's perceptions; (2) restoring the cohesion of a self diminished or destroyed by the abuse process; (3) identifying both the mechanisms of abuse and the traumatic responses to it; (4) developing self-validation and self-soothing techniques; and (5) working in therapy on the inner wounds that cause the intrusive processes.

Only when she achieves the first task—a growing sense of self—can the survivor follow the therapist's guidance in tearing away from the abusive process and maintaining distance from the flow of emotional assaults. For an emotionally abused client accustomed to anxious attachment and clinging to the abuser for life-sustaining warmth and validation, pulling away is not an option. The therapist's introduction of the concept of self-clinging, self-hugging, and self-embracing is a step toward making it a feasible one.

The disattachment process described here should be applied only to emotional abuse that occurs alone or with minimal, occasional, and non-life-threatening physical abuse. *Among some physically battered women, the growth of independence can bring new risks.* A batterer's level of rage and fear of abandonment may be so high that the woman who learns to behave more independently or discusses separation or divorce may be at risk of being murdered. Women experiencing severe physical violence should be referred to a battered women's shelter for group and individual help. Consulting or joint sessions are not appropriate until physical violence ceases. The abuser, too, should be referred to a treatment group for batterers. If the therapist chooses to work with such a couple, he or she should see the man individually within a firm context of rules regarding nonviolent behavior. Therapists working with physical abusers will find the treatment model of Men Stopping Violence (Bathrick et al., 1988) a useful guide.

Another important aspect of disattachment involves violence suffered in the past. As noted in earlier chapters, abuse experienced during childhood can leave an individual vulnerable to later emotional abuse. Current difficulties in achieving disattachment may be caused by the client's deep reluctance to give up a lifelong struggle for empathic connection with an emotionally abusive parent (or parents). Often the abusive parent met the child-victim's attempt to connect and elicit warmth with anger, distrust, aloofness, and abandonment—feelings and behavior that resulted from the parent's own problems. The abuser was connecting internally with his or her own depression and/or rage, leaving the child emotionally isolated. Years later, an abused individual may still be attempting to fill the void in her past. Clarification of this process and validation of the client's deep feelings about it are therefore crucial to successful adult therapy.

To avoid the loss and grief of giving up the past, some clients try to recapture this past by repeating the former patterns, hoping for a warmer connection but—instead—reexperiencing the trauma of earlier abandonment, negation, and desperation. Each time they yearn for and anticipate a different ending—achievement of a consistently warm and understanding connection with the partner and, through him, with the abusive parents. A survivor must experience mourning for the past and move through this pain in order to reconcile with it rather than repeating old patterns. Being trapped in and repeating past traumas gives an unchanging quality to the experience, a sense of futility and deep emotional hunger:

> O my hunger! My hunger!
> I could have gone around the world twice
> or had new children—all boys.
> It was a long trip with little days in it
> and no new places. (Sexton, 1966, p. 5)

Such emotional hunger stems from a lack of validation, joy, empathy, and meaning in human relationships. The self oppressed by its continual erosion and loneliness is a gateway to emotional starvation. One victim described how her emotional hunger presented as physical hunger:

> I felt like I was starving, which sounds crazy for a grown woman who makes a good living and can buy all the food she wants. But I'd overeat, over-drink, and feel so empty inside. It was worse when Dan was

cold and withdrawn. I yearned for him to say, "How do you feel? Oh, I understand."

Only through a therapeutic intervention that recognizes and offers an alternative to abusive attachment patterns can the victim become a survivor. In time, the victim's working through trauma and the therapist's guidance in attaining the skills of disattachment and reintegration will allow the victim to take effective action on behalf of the self and lead to a reconciliation of selves: The old self, struggling in vain to connect with abusive figures, and the new self, who can envision another mode of connection.

> Here the past and future
> Are conquered, and reconciled. (Eliot, 1966, p. 44)

The reality of emotional abuse, however, is that there is no hope of actualizing a warm and consistently empathic relation with an abuser. The survivor must disattach from this lifelong dream. At the same time, the survivor can request and insist on some degree of empathy and connection with him. Accomplishing this aim means making specific firm requests, such as, "Please listen when I tell you about my feelings, and then respond to how I feel." The real hope for a survivor is giving up one dream and adopting a new one—the dream of one's own transformation. By ending the anxious attachment she can begin new connections: "In my end is my beginning" (Eliot, 1966, p. 32).

A special problem is presented by working with victim-perpetrators in the limited time generally allowed for a court-ordered evaluation. The short evaluation does not always allow for therapeutic clarification of the role of childhood emotional deprivation or abuse. Many victim-perpetrators are themselves unaware of past abuse, and the therapist may not have access to an incarcerated victim-perpetrator to support them through the pain of recognizing childhood abuse. In these cases, a therapeutic focus on recent events is more likely to be effective.

An adult's recognition of lost warmth and attachment during childhood can cause severe grief reactions. The therapist needs to encourage clients dealing with this new information to discuss the loss of attachment and to use self-comforting techniques (such as shouting, or hitting a pillow with a plastic bat) to cope with the resulting pain and anger. The therapist can invite the client to pause during therapy to articulate the grief she felt as a lonely child, allowing the pain to emerge and expressing her anger and sadness by weeping or role-playing conversations with figures from her past.

Emotionally abused clients with a history of headaches or other somatic symptoms may find it helpful to identify body parts that are metaphors for past experiences. During therapy, for example, a client can be helped to explore feelings evoked by childhood abuse and find that her headaches are a metaphorical expression of external pounding and internal aching for connection. The therapist can invite her to express the pain by making whatever sounds she feels comfortable with. When she has a headache, Polly, an emotionally abused nurse, imagines herself as a lonely bear cub whose mother has abandoned her in the woods. She emits babylike crying sounds with her eyes closed, imagining herself as an isolated cub. Remembering emotionally abusive moments from her own childhood, she breaks into sobs. When the exercise is over, her headache has disappeared. Polly also purchased a teddy bear, which she hugs when feeling lonely. Learning to be a nurturing figure for herself was an important part of therapy, as was learning to ask her friends for support and warmth.

All symptoms should be checked medically to preclude the possibility of actual physical involvement. Headaches and other such symptoms can be caused by actual medical illness.

During disattachment, it is important for the survivor to be responsive to her abusive partner. For example, a survivor might address the abuser's fear of abandonment by explaining her actions prior to disattaching herself from some instance of abuse: "You are beginning to accuse me, and I'm going to disattach by going to the store to get some paper and books for my writing. I'll be back in a few hours." She thus fulfills her disattachment plan as well as reassuring him that she will return.

The client must make her own choice of time and circumstances to disattach, based on her increasing awareness of the effects of specific abusive behaviors and her enhanced ability to handle pain. For example, a client may choose not to disattach in the midst of an emotional assault but to confront the abuser later, when she can effectively (1) provide her own validation, (2) demonstrate ongoing confidence and self-assurance, and (3) set definite limits on the abusive process during discussions. She may, for example, tell him, "You cannot read my mind, and I do not intend to be bossy, which you are accusing me of being. But I am stating my preferences, which is very appropriate."

A therapist helping the survivor to utilize the process of disattachment should discuss this process during the second or third consultancy session, explaining disattachment and requesting the cooperation of the abusive partner. At that time the abuser's fears of abandonment can be explored, and the survivor invited to respond to them. In addition, the therapist should recommend that the survivor explain her disattachment plan to the partner, coupling it with a reassurance of her return. Survivors who do this feel they have behaved in a fair and considerate manner that precludes later feelings of guilt an abuser may attempt to evoke. The therapist can also refer an abusive person for individual therapy to work on his issues and concerns.

Reintegration

The final therapeutic modality for transforming the victim of emotional abuse into a survivor is reintegration of the self through external and internal connections. The threefold human connection with self, significant others, and community is the essence of reintegration—the change from profound loneliness and sadness to the richness of connection and the joyful embrace of life. During reintegration, the fragmented self becomes more cohesive.

An important part of the therapeutic process at all stages is the search for the client's interests, dreams, and pockets of skill, the long-dormant career wishes that inspire excitement and enthusiasm for life. The therapist should ask such questions as, "Do you have special dreams or hopes, some skill, craft, or hobby you have always wished to explore?" Most emotionally abused individuals, whose aspirations have been squashed and demeaned for some time, respond eagerly with a specific idea: photography, writing, dancing, or the like. The therapist can then direct the client toward a realistic goal. If the client cannot think of an interest, the therapist should accept this as a manifestation of the diminished self and proceed with a further discussion of interests and skills.

Working through trauma and discovering and developing new

coping skills help the client become more self-validating and better able to disattach from the abuse. Making new, interest-related connections with respectful, empathic others weaves her into an external community that makes disattachment easier. She can now turn to an external interest in place of clinging to an unresponsive and disconnected abuser. These new connections thus become the driving force of her internal and external reintegration.

Writing is a popular ambition among emotionally abused individuals, who often view it as an opportunity to express heartfelt feelings through a medium that accepts rather than denies their validity. The therapist can frequently identify a client who is well-spoken, even eloquent, and ask whether she has ever thought about writing, noting that "you seem very articulate." Many clients respond that they keep a journal or write poetry. One avenue for developing writing skills and receiving positive feedback is to approach a county or small-town newspaper and offer to write a story about a subject of local interest. Studying other stories in the publication or taking a continuing education course (at a college or university) in writing may provide an initial impetus.

Although the interests of emotional abuse survivors vary, there is no right or wrong dream. Whether it is growing flowers or going up in a hot-air balloon, any dream will do to reactivate the art of dreaming. The principal requirement is that the activity should present opportunities for (1) respectful interactions with nonabusive and caring people, (2) gaining positive feedback, and (3) generating feelings of accomplishment, excitement, and/or enchantment. It should also allow for some work at home, whether reading or working at a craft, to provide chances for the client to establish a more affirming environment. For clients whose dreaming capacities are very impaired, the therapist may need to play an active coaching role ("Have you considered learning about different kinds of roses or orchids and growing them?" "Would you be interested in trying out for the little theater? I notice they're holding open auditions." "Is volunteering for one of the agencies that help handicapped children something that would appeal to you?").

Some abused women find initiating new activities overwhelming. In these cases, the therapist can help the client break down tasks into realistic modules and plan their accomplishment, including the roles of both victim and abuser. Involving the abuser helps to ensure his cooperation. The abusive partner of a woman interested in photography, for example, can be enlisted to (1) take care of the children while she takes a photography course, (2) buy her the camera of her choice, and (3) find her some books on photography.

The therapist and the survivor need to reassure the abuser that her growth and independence do not signal separation or divorce (if indeed this is not the case). A consultancy session devoted to the new project can make him a part of the planning process rather than a barrier to its realization. It is most effective to do this after the client and therapist have held some discussion and made some plans, but still fairly early in the process. He can then serve as a consultant but not be allowed to take control of the dream or its realization. He will be asked for advice under a set of ground rules providing that (1) the survivor remains in charge of the dream; (2) she chooses how and when to express appreciation for his help; and (3) the therapist and survivor set the terms and limits of his role. In this regard, the therapist can point out to the abuser that although consultants play valuable roles, they respect the decisions and choices of the consultee.

> I decided on photography for my craft in therapy, and Gary bought me this expensive and really neat camera. When he said, "OK, Mary, listen up" and started to read the instructions to me, I reminded him that you [therapist] said how great it was of him to get it, but that I would learn to use it in the class I signed up for. I thanked him and took the camera and put it in the closet.

Mary, a television reporter, had been married to Gary for fifteen years and had experienced emotional abuse but not physical or sexual violence. Outside her job and two children, she had few interests because Gary demanded so much of her time. She responded to his jealousy with depression, feelings of loneliness, and clinging behavior. As a result of therapy, Mary took up photography as a method of external reintegration.

> Gary may have been jealous of my attention to the camera that evening. When I began talking about it, he started sighing and complaining—the usual prelude to abuse. I started to come apart but said to myself, "You are just fine." To Gary I said, "Excuse me, I need to disattach. I'll run upstairs and study my photography book." Two hours

later, when I came back downstairs, he seemed normal. It was the first time I had ever escaped from the play-by-play, always-the-same humiliation. Before that I would always grab hold and want to talk, and when he wouldn't I would cry, et cetera, et cetera, et cetera. But this time I felt so good and powerful.

Mary's experience demonstrates the need of the emotionally abused person for internal reintegration—cohesion of the self. The disintegration of the self has damaged her internal sense of validity about her own ideas, perceptions, and personality, making it difficult to cope with the nightmares, painful memories, and flashbacks that are characteristic of trauma. Mary described her sense of disintegration in the relationship with Gary:

> I begin to fragment, to break up inside into little pieces. It is as if he had a chisel and is chipping away at the core of me. I get where I can't think of the right word, and I'm not able to string a few ideas together, which is really bad when I'm live on television. I started keeping a mirror with me so that if I feel like I've disappeared, I can sneak a close-up look during the commercial breaks of newscasts. I don't know what I'd do if my lines weren't scripted. I just read the words on the air.

Repeated experiences of losing vital parts of the self are a powerful stimulus for grief, confusion, and depression. Even so, most emotionally abused women are unaware of their self-loss until they learn to recognize it in therapy. Some cannot look at themselves in a mirror or accept a compliment. Instead they attempt to avoid confronting their deep sense of emptiness and worthlessness. Others, like Mary, need to look at a mirror to assure themselves of their own existence.

For these clients, the primary goals of internal reintegration are (1) to restore cohesion to the inner self, (2) to provide mechanisms for its continued protection, and (3) to create opportunities for transformation. To help her identify various components of the self, the therapist can ask the client to list her self-parts by giving them names—enthusiasm, intelligence, athletic ability, and so on— and assigning them functions within the total self. Naming them makes these components more real and alive for the client. During an emotional assault, she can learn to remember and interact with the parts that help her toward self-validation and disattachment.

This tool should only be initiated if the client feels comfortable with it, which should be evident after six to eight weeks of therapy.

Together, therapist and client can develop and "Intrapsychic Council" in which these aspects of herself learn skills of interaction, mutual respect, reality assessment, decision-making, self-forgiveness, connectedness, and celebration. Rather than reacting only to the abuse, the survivor enlists the self-parts to help her deal with the abuser and her own responses. One self-part might help another figure out what to do when abuse occurs, helping create a more cohesive response to stress. *This technique of therapy should only be used, however, after the therapist has ruled out the possibility of Multiple Personality Disorder* (APA, 1987, pp. 269–272). Individuals suffering from this disorder would be at risk of further confusion if this method were used.

Other survivors, however, find this a useful tool for developing and maintaining self-cohesion. The therapist helped Mary develop her own inner council:

> My list includes "B.G.," which stands for "Big Girl." She's the part of me that always gets to the television station on time, dresses right, and stuff like that. Then there is "P.Q.," a whimsical and mischievous scoundrel who plays tricks on people and is fun, and she comes across in my twinkling eyes on air and the way I tease my coanchor. "Josie" is my sad part and lonely, too, since I was a little girl and Mom died. "Balloons" is the happy part of me, excitable and enthusiastic, the part that I thought died during my marriage with Gary. But no, she is back and with real hope.

The Intrapsychic Council can be an effective way to gain the skills crucial to reintegration: decision-making, self-nurturing, and self-forgiveness. In Mary's case, the council cooperated in decision-making; it was "Balloons" who took her away into another room or to a friend's house when Gary started being abusive. This self-nurturing system thus provided a mechanism for emotional safety. It has also assisted her efforts at self-validation and disattachment:

> My part I call Josie said, "Enough sadness already." Balloons floated me away with B.G. at the wheel when I asked Gary to stop criticizing me and he wouldn't, or couldn't. I took my camera and shot a lot of good pictures on the way to my friend's house. I actually didn't think at

all about what Gary said, with the confusion that always goes with that yucky process. I felt connected to myself and really hopeful that the newspaper would print some of my photographs. I have an appointment with an editor next week to show him my pictures and a few stories I wrote.

Mary spent four weeks in individual therapy, as well as many hours of homework, creating awareness of the valued parts of her personality and naming her council members. The therapist cautioned her to keep information about the members within the therapeutic setting to prevent abuse of the developing parts before she had learned self-protective skills. The therapist's participation in the process included mentioning Mary's characteristics and asking questions like, "Do you think your sense of humor merits a part in your self-system?" The therapist also suggested that Mary assign one member of the council to reassure her husband that disattachment did not mean abandoning him. Gary mentioned his appreciation of this reassurance many times.

Part of her transformation is fulfilled by developing the Intrapsychic Council or some other method of getting to know and appreciate her parts. The process creates its own sense of cohesiveness and integration. During the process of reintegration, emotionally abused women usually express an increase in hope—a result of their realistic perception that while the abuser may not have changed drastically, their own growth is very real, potentially joyful, and laden with future possibilities. Mary's submission to the newspaper editor resulted in publication of a story and two photographs. Now, in addition to her television reporting job, she has become a free-lance photographer and is excited about her skills and growing sense of self: "There is something so exciting about creating pictures and stories around my own perceptions and ideas. It's a lot different from reporting other people's stories. And I feel so much more whole and happy with myself."

For survivors like Mary, the goals of internal and external reintegration are self-connection, connections with caring others, and connection with the larger world through sharing skills, accomplishments, and social concerns. As the survivor experiences self-connection, she feels more fully alive and optimistic, delighted with her self and her accomplishments. And as her self-image improves, her sense of trust in her ability to think, analyze, and create grows. She experiences a sense of empowerment when she sets limits and protects herself in relationships. While the self-connection emphasizes awareness, appreciation, and enjoyment of her own feelings, ideas, and dreams, it does not preclude the warm responsiveness to others that is crucial to human relationships. Establishing more consistently empathic connections helps her know others and be known and enjoyed by them. At the same time, external reintegration activities—like Mary's photography—become ways to get in touch with the self and to receive positive feedback from the community.

The return of humor, a stronger self, and a transformed sense of newness are all hallmarks of reconnection with the self. One client, herself a therapist, jokingly remarked that, by introducing her to the Intrapsychic Council, "You are helping me develop a 'consciously adaptive, multiple personality nondisorder.' And I feel strong and new." Mary laughed when she described her whimsical self-part named Balloons: "I imagine the helium-filled balloons lifting me up above the abusive process. I hang onto the balloon strings and am transported to peace and self-confidence."

Yet even in the midst of the excitement of mastering self-validation and disattachment, some survivors experience the occasional return of hopelessness and confusion. Such feelings are realistic for survivors who remain in an abusive relationship whose repetitive pattern is impossible to break. Indeed, attachment to such a process *is* hopeless. When the therapist identifies this root cause of hopelessness, most clients become less confused and are able to redirect their hopes realistically toward their own growth, whatever moments of empathic connection with their partners they can achieve, and the widening circle of connection with the outside world.

During individual and consulting interviews with the abuser, steps can be taken to decrease the emotional abuse, although it seldom stops completely. In some cases, however, the pattern of abuse is disrupted because (1) the abuser decreases the emotional violence; (2) the survivor is able to self-validate and point out occasional lapses to the abuser; and/or (3) the survivor disattaches from the abuse and reintegrates during its occurrence, short-circuiting her own anxious attachment and clinging behavior. Thus, even in the face of emotional abuse, the survivor's skills of self-validation, disattachment, and reintegration alter the entire process. The flow of abuse is curtailed when the survivor manages to separate from the assaults with a sense of hope and self-cohesion.

The growth curve is likely to be a jagged one, with recurrences of difficulties because of illness, loss of job or loved one, or other stresses. The survivor may have problems maintaining self-validation, utilizing the Intrapsychic Council, controlling intrusive imagery, avoiding anxious clinging, and/or staying involved with her chosen activity. It is important to predict such events for clients, reassuring them that these difficulties will become less frequent and intense over time. The therapist should offer to be available to clients, by telephone or in person, during periods of crisis, validating the courage it takes to get through such pain and arrive at the transforming ray of hope at the end of the tunnel. A crisis may even become a turning point for additional growth (Roberts, 1984). When therapy is terminated, the therapist should invite the client to return if and when she encounters renewed difficulties.

Dr. Marolyn Wells suggests that whatever therapeutic interventions people experience, individuals come to therapy with different personalities and motivations for growth; thus, it is important for some emotional abuse survivors to continue therapy that addresses their unique needs for additional growth. Differences in desired directions for growth may serve as indicators for which therapeutic modality would be most effective. (Wells, personal communication, Feb. 1994).

The joy of reconnecting with the self and discovering new aspects of connections with others is a cause for celebration. Therapists can model an appropriate appreciation for the survivor's accomplishments, helping her experience the celebrations as hallmarks in the growth and transformation of her self. Using the term *survivor* connotes a new level of functioning, a step forward. Mary, however, suggested that the term *survival* did not quite fit her feelings of excitement and sense of accomplishment: "The term should be *celebrating survivor* or *emotional survivor*, or maybe it should be *celebrating emotional survivor*." A male survivor, whose story is told in the Epilogue, describes feeling newly alive, in contrast to the terror and "deadness" he felt in his emotionally abusive marriage. For Jerry, the decision about staying with an abusive partner is clear: To sustain their happiness and be free from the "fear of being emotionally attacked . . . having always to be vigilant," all emotionally abused individuals should leave the relationship.

Mary, in contrast, speaks wistfully of her love for Gary. She enjoys being with him some of the time and sharing interests in travel and sports. She plans to keep growing and to remain married to him. In the final analysis, such decisions must always be made by the client. The therapist can point out possibilities and realities, as well as help the client to find empowering means of transformation and to make mutually empathic connections.

The therapeutic journey with emotional abuse survivors is a rewarding one for both client and therapist. Many emotionally abused individuals are sensitive, creative people; their external reintegration can yield fascinating accomplishments. Attaining the opportunity to grow and flourish creates a very different environment from the one in which they were demeaned. Their renewed excitement about life and its possibilities is at the heart of the therapeutic process.

Epilogue

Other Targets of Emotional Abuse

Heterosexual women are not the sole targets of emotional abuse. Children, older adults, lesbians, gay men, adolescents, college students, heterosexual men, and prostitutes may all suffer from this form of interpersonal violence. It can occur in the home, the workplace, or even in the classroom.

No matter what the victim's age, sex, economic status, ethnic background, education, sexual orientation, or religion, the experience of emotional abuse is universal. The characteristic pattern, mechanisms, and levels of emotional abuse are the same. Its primary consequence is always a painful erosion of the self. The same effects on the victim's emotional and physical well-being described for emotionally abused women in heterosexual relationships—from loneliness, depression, somatic problems, proneness to accidents, eating disorders, diminished capacities, and substance abuse to murder, suicide, and the victim-perpetrator syndrome—beset other victims.

This epilogue can only touch on some of the particular features of emotional abuse suffered by lesbians, children, and heterosexual men. Each of these groups, as well as older adults, adolescents, and gay men, needs to be studied in their own right. In the meantime, because the effects of emotional abuse *are* universal, therapists working with these clients can effectively apply the therapeutic model described in Chapter 6.

Lesbians

"Walking on eggshells all the time" is Linda's description of life with her emotionally abusive lover. Linda, a twenty-six-year-old student, recently separated from Janet after a long relationship during which she felt continuously labeled and put down: "I never knew if she really liked me, because she would constantly correct me. She claimed I chewed like a cow, yelled at me for leaving the oven on, and said I walked too heavily." When cooking at Janet's house, Linda repeatedly forgot to turn off the oven, something she never did at home. It happened, she explained, "because I was always so frazzled by her. She was constantly looking for things I did wrong." Janet even claimed that that Linda ate too loudly: "She retrained my way of eating. I still chew differently, more slowly. That's a legacy of the relationship."

No matter what the situation, Janet always seemed to consider other peoples' needs and wishes to be more important than Linda's. For example, she complained that Linda was noisy when she got up during the night and that this bothered Janet's male roommate, who was ill with AIDS. When Linda came back to bed Janet would elbow her angrily, not quite raising a bruise but hurting her nonetheless. Linda sometimes suffered asthma attacks during the night and woke up wheezing; instead of sympathizing, Janet reacted angrily to being disturbed. Even when her roommate was away visiting his parents, Janet seemed to be mad at Linda most of the time.

Linda remembers wistfully how Janet showered affection on her dog—more than she did on Linda. When she and Janet first became friends, however, Janet complimented Linda a good deal, saying things like, "You are pretty and smart." Soon after they became lovers the compliments stopped, and Janet began her campaign of criticism. This verbal abuse, which began in a clear and overt manner, later went "underground and become more subtle and covert."

Barbara Hart (1986) has described the mechanisms of emotional abuse in lesbian relationships, including

> humiliation, degradation; lying; isolation; selection of entertainment/ friends/religious experience; telling the partner that she is crazy, dumb, ugly; withholding critical information; selecting the food the partner eats; bursts of fury; pouting or withdrawal; mind manipulation. (p. 189)

In her relationship with Janet, Linda experienced several of these overt and covert mechanisms of abuse and suffered the resultant erosion of her sense of self.

Linda's description of the relationship also contains some of the components of psychological torture, which Amnesty International enumerates as "isolation, induced debility (sleep and food deprivation), monopolization of perceptions, verbal degradation (denial of powers, humiliation), hypnosis, drugs, threats to kill, occasional indulgences (positives: verbal or material)" (Amnesty International, 1975). Like the tortured prisoners of tyrannical governments, Linda experienced sleep deprivation, verbal degradation, and isolation, but only occasional "indulgences" of warmth. Janet also attempted to "monopolize" Linda's perceptions, substituting her own view of reality as if it were the only valid one; as the relationship developed, she increased her degrading criticisms.

Eventually Linda broke up with Janet "to save face" when the latter became involved in another relationship and told her about it. Linda felt "shattered":

> My self-confidence is still not where I want it to be. I had low self-confidence beforehand, but I had been in therapy and improved it some. Janet didn't like me to be around other people much, but now I am back in touch with my friends. I still miss the occasional warmth we shared.

Currently, in therapy, Linda is building a stronger sense of self and reports feeling much happier. She is working on regaining a view of herself as a likable and lovable person. Perhaps most important, she is struggling to "figure myself out" and learning to relate to others in a different way:

> There is something that was not here before, almost like a physical presence that helps me keep inside my own boundary, to stay separate. The physical presence is me—it's my boundary and it doesn't allow anyone else to enter my selfness until I know it's safe.

Linda's story demonstrates the consistency of the patterns, mechanisms, and levels of emotional abuse, regardless of the gender of either the abuser or the victim. Nonetheless, there are some important differences. Pharr (1986) points out that "the battered non-lesbian experiences violence within the context of a misogynist world; the lesbian experiences violence within the context of a world that is not only woman-hating but is also homophobic. And that is a great difference" (p. 204). Pharr identifies two types of *ho-*

mophobia, which she defines as "fear, dread, or hatred of homosexuals" (p. 206). *External* homophobia is a weapon used by the dominant society to punish men and women who have broken with the "system of male dominance (by loving the same sex, by exhibiting behavior that is out of line with traditional sex-roles)" (p. 206). *Internal* homophobia, in contrast, involves the homosexual's own belief that "others are justified in their prejudices, when we believe there is something wrong with us, when we feel we do not deserve equality and freedom, and when we take in the world's view and suffer from low self-esteem and self-hatred" (pp. 206–207).

Thus lesbians or gay men, who repeatedly experience homophobic degradation and abasement in the general society, are especially at risk for involvement in emotionally abusive relationships. They already suffer from a lack of relational validation because of the discounting and negative labeling of external homophobia. When they internalize the homophobia, the resulting low self-esteem and self-hatred make them vulnerable to added emotional abuse from a partner. They may even feel that they deserve the abuse.

Lesbians, who receive society's message of general external homophobia, also suffer, as Pharr acknowledges, simply from being women. Pharr describes still-pervasive cultural beliefs hold that women are weaker, less able and intelligent, and less suited to handling the important business of the world than are men. Moreover, women who choose not to marry (whether lesbian or heterosexual) tend to be pictured as less attractive and somehow a threat to society. In spite of recent changes in these traditional attitudes, only women who perform the crucial tasks of bearing and nurturing children are likely to receive society's full respect and approbation. Lesbians, like heterosexual women who do not bear children, have often internalized this cultural message—one that can make them feel less worthy as people and, hence, more vulnerable to emotional abuse.

Children

The emotional abuse of children is an underrecognized problem in our society, one that has tremendous consequences. The damage suffered by emotionally abused children is both compelling and tragic because these victims are likely to repeat the abusive pattern with their own children. Many adult victims and emotional abusers have a history of harsh emotional abuse as children. It is thus doubly important for therapists to identify and intervene in this form of violence.

Children are frequently emotionally abused in public. Not long ago in an ice cream parlor I saw a woman slap a little girl about six years old very hard and call her "dumb one." The other ten adults waiting for ice cream were silently horrified. They stared at the mother and said nothing. I approached the abusive mother and commented, "Isn't it hard being a mom these days?" I then looked at the child and said, "It isn't easy being a child, either." The mother started to cry. "My husband left me last night," she blurted out. "I don't know how I'm going to manage. I'm so scared."

I gave the mother a family service agency card displaying a telephone number she could use to request help and asked if it would be useful. I assured her that there was no waiting list. The mother's response was immediate and intense: "I'll go home and call them right away. I can drive and I have a car, so I can go in to see them anytime. Maybe they'll see me this afternoon." After she left, several customers who had witnessed the slap and the emotional assault gathered to discuss them. They commented on the awkwardness of the situation and how bewildered they felt about the right thing to do. One of them commented that the child appeared more distressed by being called "dumb" than by being slapped.

Whether it occurs in public or in the home, the emotional abuse of children involves overt and covert levels of abuse and the same mechanisms used in adult violence. Because of their natural dependence on the nurturing adult, children cannot escape abuse and are highly vulnerable to anxious attachment, which binds them closely to their abusive parents.

The emotional abuse of children has been principally analyzed as a form of psychological maltreatment. Garbarino, Guttmann, and Seeley (1989) have identified and traced five principal components of abuse suffered by infants, small children, school-age children, and adolescents:

• Rejection or emotional abandonment
• Terror
• Ignoring the child

- Isolation
- Corruption

Rejection of infants occurs when a parent refuses to "touch or show affection to the child or to acknowledge the child's accomplishments" (p. 25). It is characterized by "behaviors that communicate or constitute abandonment" (p. 25). A caretaker may reject an infant's attachment by refusing to return smiles and vocalizations, by leaving him or her alone for long periods of time, or simply by abandoning the child to another's care.

During the child's early years, an abandoning caretaker may exclude the child from family activities and refuse the child's attempts to hug and develop ties of affection. Later, an emotionally abusive parent is likely to communicate a consistently negative self-image to the child by labeling him "dumb" or "wicked" or "ugly," belittling his accomplishments, and/or using him as a scapegoat. A parent may refuse to acknowledge the changing role of an adolescent—continuing to treat her like a young child, verbally humiliating her, excessively criticizing her, or even expelling her from the family home.

Children and adolescents treated in this way often develop life-long patterns of repeated attempts to master such rejections. Lennie, the wife of an emotionally abusive man, recalled her own parents' behavior:

> My father always called me "dumbhead." He would shake his head and wonder how he had raised such a rude and mean child. This occurred even when, at age five and six, I was knocking myself out to be polite. My mother didn't like me to touch her; hugs were out of the question. She was always worried about the next party and what she would wear. I can hardly believe I suffer the same name-calling and rejection from my husband.

Many such emotionally needy children keep trying to please unresponsive nurturers, hoping desperately that the latter will finally respond with warmth. Others withdraw in anger and frustration or, indulging in self-blame, search within themselves for the heinous faults that merit this treatment. Such internalized rejection takes a heavy toll of the child's developing self, leading to a poor self-image and low self-esteem.

According to Garbarino et al. (1989), the other four components of emotional abuse follow a similar pattern of keeping the child mentally and emotionally off-balance and isolated from more benign influences. Some emotionally abusing parents utilize terror, "threatening the child with extreme or vague but sinister punishment, intentionally stimulating intense fear, creating a climate of unpredictable threat, or setting unmeetable expectations and punishing the child for not meeting them" (p. 25). A parent who ignores the child is "psychologically unavailable . . . preoccupied with self and unable to respond to the child's behaviors" (p. 26).

A mild form of isolating the child occurs when parents fail to provide normal opportunities for social interaction. The moderate form contains active efforts to avoid social interaction and may develop into a severe form in which "the parent thwarts all efforts by the child and others to make contact" (p. 27). Lastly, one of the most extreme components of adult emotional abuse of a child occurs when a parent actively corrupts the child. He or she may reinforce antisocial or deviant behavior, encourage delinquency, or even create and sustain such risky behavioral patterns as drug addiction, criminal actions, and sex abuse.

Wanda, a seven-year-old girl referred for therapy because of school problems, presented as a quiet child who clung anxiously to her mother and sucked her thumb. Sarah, her mother, complained that Wanda cried before going to school each day and was failing in her class. Her teacher informed the therapist that Wanda was withdrawn, fatigued, and distracted much of the time. She sometimes fell asleep at her desk.

During therapy, Wanda revealed that her mother's boyfriend sold drugs out of their home; he occasionally asked Wanda to deliver them to people living in the apartment complex. When the therapist broached the subject of sexual abuse by the boyfriend, Wanda indicated that it was not occurring. Sarah, who was working twelve hours a day, readily admitted that "I have no time to be bothered with Wanda. Quite honestly," she complained, "she's a bother and a stupid child." Wanda was aware of her mother's feelings toward her:

My mom says I'm stupid. Her boyfriend Stephen says the only smart thing I do is help him take drugs around. I know it's not right. I'm scared when people stare at me while I'm taking the drugs around. I can't sleep at night. I'm so tired at school. At home, Mom and Stephen say mean things, like I'm skinny and smelly. And I feel like I'd be better off dead than bugging them. That's what they say. My mom won't hug me. I'm not supposed to go out and play. I sneak out sometimes. Sometimes I wish I was dead.

Stephen had been under surveillance by law enforcement officials and was arrested just after a therapy session that included Wanda, Sarah, Sarah's aunt Susan, and Stephen. After the arrest, Sarah told the therapist she did not have time to take care of Wanda alone. Sarah's aunt Susan, who lived nearby and had a child the same age as Wanda, had earlier expressed a wish for Wanda to live with her. When the therapist pursued this idea, Sarah, Susan, and Wanda all agreed to the new living arrangement. Wanda moved in with her great-aunt and continued with individual therapy. Her therapist occasionally scheduled a family session in which Wanda's mother, great-aunt, and cousin all participated. Wanda reported feeling happier and freer, and her school grades rose from all F's to A's and B's as she worked in therapy on developing a more positive self-image.

A review of the literature suggests that children who experience emotional abuse present with multiple emotional and behavioral problems (S. Hart, Germain, & Brassard, 1987). Those who internalize the abuse become depressed, suicidal, and withdrawn. They manifest self-destructiveness, depression, suicidal thoughts, passivity, withdrawal (avoidance of social contacts), shyness, and a low degree of communication with others (Junewicz, 1983, p. 61). They are likely to have low self-esteem (Egeland, Stroufe, & Erikson, 1983; Jacoby, 1985) and may suffer from feelings of guilt and remorse, depression, loneliness, rejection, and resignation. Perceiving themselves as unworthy and the world as a hostile place in which they are bound to fail, many are unwilling to try new tasks or develop new skills. They have difficulty visualizing and planning for the future. Emotionally abused children have nightmares, nervous habits, and suffer from such somatic complaints as headaches (Aber & Zigler, 1981; Fontana, 1973; Krugman & Krugman, 1984). They may exhibit passive-aggressive behavior at home and at school.

Some other children who externalize abuse act out by mistreating animals or by emotionally or physically abusing younger siblings. They may be unpredictable and violent, their behavior characterized by impulsive action rather than conformity to social norms (Fontana, 1973; Rohner & Rohner, 1980). They "frequently become anxious, aggressive, and hostile. They suffer from constant fear and feel ready to 'hit back'" (Garbarino et al., 1989, p. 61). Emotionally abused adolescents have become truants, runaways, destructive, depressed, and suicidal.

Therapists working with children should routinely screen them for emotional, sexual, and physically abusive histories. Whatever the techniques used to gain information, make diagnoses, and establish treatment plans, the underlying process of emotional abuse must be uncovered. A traumatized child, grieving from the loss of warm connection from a rejecting parental figure, may be unable to reveal the abuse immediately and directly. Utilizing clay work, art therapy, play therapy, or some other technique can help the therapist identify the abusive persons in the child's life, whether they are siblings, friends, neighbors, relatives, or parents. In severe cases, the therapist will need to report emotional abuse to protective agencies. In these cases, the therapist should exercise clinical judgment about such reporting procedures, for even moderate emotional abuse can be harmful to children.

It is important to recognize that children can be emotionally abused not only by parents and other caretakers but also by siblings. When this happens, the child tends to feel inadequate and out of place in the family system (Rohner & Rohner, 1980; Whiting, 1976). Wiehe (1991) described one adult victim who struggled with her sister's labels of "dumb," "stupid," and "fat" (p. 42). In her forties, she was still attempting to prove her worth to herself. Wiehe views this kind of emotional abuse as "the most common type of sibling abuse, and among the most destructive." Because of the close relationship, "victims believe the names they are called and the ridicule and degrading comments directed at them. Sadly . . . the abuse becomes a self-fulfilling prophesy for its victims" (pp. 42–43).

In therapy, children should be helped to recognize the specific abusive processes they experience. The therapist and young victim need to discuss the child's reactions to abuse in individual sessions. It is also valuable to have occasional family sessions to uncover pockets of support for the child within the family and identify additional sources of abuse. Consultation with teachers can be helpful in assessing behavior and gaining support for the child.

Two useful components of treatment for emotionally abused children and adolescents are (1) activities shared by the therapist and the child, and (2) establishment of important secondary supports. Sharing activities that establish bonds of affection will increase children's self-esteem; and connections with the therapist and other supportive people can encourage self-development. In addition, the therapist may obtain important diagnostic information on these occasions. It is often easier for the child to reveal distressing experiences while riding in a car or engaged in an activity that mitigates the intensity of emotional pain.

During some of Wanda's sessions, the therapist took her to an ice skating rink. There she met an instructor who agreed to give her lessons in return for cleaning up around the rink on weekends. Wanda often talked about these activities:

> You know, I fall down on the ice sometimes. You [therapist] don't yell or say I'm ugly and clumsy. Stephen and my mom do. You say I'm brave when I get up. It's true. I am brave. But I never knew it. And you're right. I am graceful. I think I'll be a dancer. The skating teacher says I'm graceful, too. Wow! Me graceful!

It has been suggested that emotionally abusive parents have fewer supports and poorer coping skills than other parents (Hickox & Furnell, 1989). They may handle their child's difficult behavior ineffectively or may simply abandon the attempt after trying a mix of unproductive child-rearing practices. Abusive parents' inability to cope with stress in various forms is another part of this pattern. When, for example, the therapist encouraged Wanda's mother to enroll her in a modern dance class (in addition to the skating lessons), Sarah found the search for a dance studio stressful and frustrating. With the support and praise of the therapist and her aunt, however, Sarah followed through and succeeded in finding Wanda a dance instructor.

Secondary relationships that include support and positive regard for the child have the potential of making a significant and lasting difference in a child's life. Warm and validating connections—uninterrupted by the disconnections of emotional abuse—are valuable learning experiences for these children. These experiences can enhance the child's self-esteem, provide opportunities for growth, and possibly stimulate later career choice. In Wanda's case, the dance instructor became an important influence in her life. With the help of this mentor, Wanda was able to spend many summers in another state at a dance camp. Later she attended a college specializing in dance. Her talent and enthusiasm enabled Wanda to obtain various scholarships and grants to finance her dancing.

Wanda's successful history suggests that, while most traditional psychotherapy takes place during formal sessions in an office, therapists can connect with parents and children and share therapeutic concepts in a variety of settings. Interactions can take place in a public place where emotional and/or physical violence unexpectedly occurs; in a courtroom where emotionally abused children and adults are involved in conflict; or in a television studio providing informed news commentary and support of community education projects. In these and other settings, therapists can both confront and support abusive adults, suggest different child-rearing practices, and offer them and the general public a different model of caring for the children. Finally, therapists can support the use of such recreational opportunities as camp, girl scouts, and special interest groups like sports teams and dance classes that provide children the chance to experience warm connections with nonabusive adults.

Men

Most writers contend that "the effects of abuse are equally profound whether the victim is male or female; they are also generally similar" (Lew, 1990, p. 38). However, because women have grown up in a society in which they are expected to be

> passive, weaker, powerless beings, there is room for sympathy when they are victimized. Again, this does not mean that female victims have an easier time of it. (On the contrary, the very acceptance of victimization of women perpetuates abuse and inhibits their recovery.) But there is a particular focus of the problem that is faced only by men. It arises

from the fact that our culture provides no room for a man as victim. Men are simply not supposed to be victimized. A "real man" is expected to be able to protect himself in any situation. (p. 41)

Lew's work with survivors of incest suggests that society's unwillingness to see men as victims can cause them to believe that they must either avenge or internalize their suffering. Men who grow up believing that it is unacceptable to admit hurt, to cry, or to be vulnerable, Lew argues, miss crucial experiences; they fail to develop the skills they need to participate fully in mutually empathic connections. As boys and men, they learn to "wall off" parts of their experience rather than sharing them with a partner. Both society and men themselves perceive vulnerability in relationships as a weakness. This perception—shared by both heterosexual and gay men—often leads to isolation and an inability to create a mutually interdependent bond among men who yearn to share tenderness and intimacy.

Jerry is a forty-two-year-old heterosexual college student. He was emotionally abused as a child and as an adult. He wrote the following "Notes of an Emotionally Abused Man" in an effort to recall, and to help him overcome, the pain he suffered. He gave me the notes to include in this book as a gift, in hopes that they will contribute to the recognition that men experience emotional abuse involving the same mechanisms and levels of abuse as other victims. In Jerry's view, men's hesitation to acknowledge emotional abuse and seek help for it stems from fear of being seen as a "wimp."

Notes of an Emotionally Abused Man

I have no childhood memories of my relationship with my parents before the age of five. Of the time before that, I have only two recurring unpleasant images but no verbal memories. My verbal recollection begins with our move to the farm a week before my sixth birthday.

I remember my mother telling me I was worthless: "You'll never amount to a hill of beans. You're not worth the salt in your gravy. I'm so ashamed of you." She was always wondering, with hatred in her voice, "What did I ever do to deserve you?" I don't know what I did to make her hate me so much. No matter what I did, it was wrong; nothing pleased her. I tried to stay out of her way and be as quiet as possible.

She used to threaten to whip me with a belt until she raised blisters and then break the blisters and rub salt in them. She never actually did this, but on more than one occasion she left welts on my legs. She said the welts were my fault because I didn't stand still while she whipped me. As she spanked me, she repeated over and over, "Hold still, hold still."

When I was a sophomore in high school I was the fastest runner in my gym class, and the track coach wanted me to go out for the team. But when I asked my dad to sign the insurance release form, he refused. He said I should consider myself lucky to be going to high school at all. He never had a chance to go, and all he kept saying was "Just be thankful you are getting to go to high school."

My sister used to do things and blame them on me. My mother would question us and then punish me for something I hadn't done. When we were grown up, my sister admitted all the things she had done that I was whipped for. My mother asked, "Why, Elizabeth?" but my sister just laughed. It wasn't funny to me, even after all those years.

Somehow, it seemed, my parents and my sister didn't want me to have any joy in my life. When I was eighteen years old, my mom and my sister conspired to break me up with my girlfriend. The insurance for my car was in my sister's name, and she threatened to cancel it if I drove after 10:00 P.M. She knew that my girlfriend didn't get off work until 11:00 P.M. This is the kind of thing that made me join the army when I was eighteen; I stayed away from home until I was twenty-five.

About that time my wife and I were married in California at a little chapel overlooking the Pacific Ocean. After three months of marriage she insisted on separate bedrooms. She said I didn't know how to sleep, that only she and her mom knew how to sleep right. When we visited her parents, she would sleep with her mother, while I slept on another queen-size bed in the room, either alone or, after my son's birth, with him.

At this time we were both working and saving money to buy a house. Each of us would save out twenty five dollars a week from our pay to buy lunch and for a little "mad money." Once I saved my "mad money" and bought her a dozen roses. "I don't want no damn roses, I want a house," she stormed at me. Even when I explained that I'd bought the roses by saving my "mad money," she still insisted I should have added it to what we were saving for the house.

When we built the house, she picked out the floor plan. She picked out the lot, the Formica for the countertops, the linoleum, the dining room chandelier, the bathroom mirror, the commode, the sink—everything. She chose the carpeting and the sliding doors to the patio. Yet within ninety days after we moved in, she was unhappy because someone else had a larger, nicer house than we did.

After our son was born she threatened to divorce me and take the baby away if everything wasn't done her way. She was just like my mother. Nothing I did pleased her. The more I did, the more she complained. She increased the ridicule and put-downs. She taught my son to call me Dummy. Her favorite names for me were Dummy and Wimp.

Even in public she would say things like she wished she'd never married me. That confused me because I didn't think I was such a bad person; but she sure made me feel like I was. I tried everything I could to please her, but nothing made her happy.

She even threatened to kill me while I was sleeping, or to castrate me. I would stack books between the door and the foot of my bed so she couldn't get in my room at night. I can still hear the evil laugh she gave if she tried the door and found it barricaded.

Twice she pulled a knife on me—because she was angry about my eating. I had altered my diet to help with my allergies and breathing problems, and it made her mad. I could go out and work all day and breathe fine, but I would have an asthma attack within an hour of coming home. I lost a lot of weight, too. When we were married I weighed 151 pounds; within two and a half years I was down to 120. As long as I was married to her I couldn't gain any weight.

After I lost the weight she said I was skinny and ugly. According to her I had the world's ugliest upper lip, and she asked me to grow a moustache. I grew a moustache for her. Then she said my jaws were sunken in and I should grow a beard to hide my ugly face. I grew a beard for her. Still, she refused to walk with me in public; she claimed she was ashamed to be seen with me. She either walked ahead of me or behind me, but never with me.

There were times when she would refuse to talk to me. At other times, she blamed me for things I had no control over, like her own swearing. Sometimes she would ask me a question and then turn and walk away and ignore my answer. At first, I would follow her and try to talk to her, but I soon learned it was useless and just left her alone when she did this.

I never knew what she was going to do next. Whatever it was, it was usually negative. She committed very few positive acts and made almost no positive statements all the time we were married. Our relationship was almost totally devoid of human kindness. We had sex only when she wanted it. She used to say, "If you want sex this month, be in my room in five minutes. And you had better be ready." When I left for work in the morning, there was no hug, no kiss. Not even a handshake or a kind word. Usually she would say, "Sell something, we need the money."

Many times I would drive to the cemetery in the morning to read, pray, and cry, trying to gain enough composure to face a customer with a smile instead of looking sad and depressed. (I sold Bibles.) I used to wonder why God made me so unlovable. What had I done to deserve this? At times I had suicidal thoughts. I guess my religion kept me from acting on them.

I finally realized there was nothing I could ever do to please her. I was never more lonesome or alone than in the eight years we were married. It seemed that no one stood behind me but my shadow. After it was all over, I felt she had never bothered to get to know me at all. She was too busy trying to destroy me. I wonder what she gained from it all.

References

Aber, J. L., & Zigler, E. (1981). Developmental considerations in the definition of child maltreatment. In R. Rizley & D. Cicchetti (Eds.), *Developmental perspectives on child maltreatment* (New Directions for Child Development, no. 11). San Francisco: Jossey-Bass.

American Psychiatric Association. (1987). *Diagnostic and statistical manual of mental disorders* (rev. 3rd ed.) Washington, DC: American Psychiatric Association.

Amnesty International (1975). *Amnesty International: Report on torture.* New York: Farrar, Straus, and Giroux.

Bathrick, D., Carlin, K., Kaufman, G., Jr., & Vodde, R. (1988). *Men stopping violence: A program for change.* Atlanta: Men Stopping Violence, Inc.

Borkowski, M., Murch, M., & Walker, V. (1983). *Marital violence: The community response.* London: Tavistock.

Bowlby, J. (1973). *Attachment and loss, vol. 2: Separation, anxiety, and anger.* New York: Basic Books.

Bowlby, J. (1979). *The making and breaking of affectional bonds.* New York: Tavistock/Routledge.

Bowlby, J. (1988). *A secure base: Parent-child attachment and healthy human development.* New York: Basic Books.

Browne, A. (1989). *When battered women kill.* New York: Free Press.

Cook, D., & Cook, A. (1984). A systematic treatment approach to wife battering. *Journal of Marital and Family Therapy, 10,* 83–93.

Douglas, M. A. (1987). The battered woman syndrome. In D. J. Sonkin (Ed.), *Domestic violence on trial: Psychological and legal dimensions of family violence* (pp. 39–54). New York: Springer.

Dutton, D., & Painter, S. L. (1981). Traumatic bonding: The development of emotional attachments in battered women and other relationships of intermittent abuse. *Victimology: An International Journal, 6,* 139–155.

Egeland, B., Stroufe, A., & Erikson, M. (1983). The developmental consequences of different patterns of maltreatment. *Child Abuse and Neglect, 7,* 459–469.

Eliot, T. S. (1966). *Four quartets.* London: Faber & Faber.

Everstine, D., & Everstine, L. (1983). *People in crisis: Strategic therapeutic interventions.* New York: Brunner/Mazel.

127

Ewing, C. P. (1987). *Battered women who kill: Psychological self-defense as legal justification*. Lexington, MA: Lexington.

Ewing, C. P. (1990). Psychological self-defense. *Law and Human Behavior, 14,* 579–594.

Ferraro, K. J. (1979). Physical and emotional battering: Aspects of managing hurt. *California Sociologist, 2,* 134–149.

Follingstad, D. R., & Neckerman, A. P. (1988). Reactions to victimization and coping strategies of battered women: The ties that bind. *Clinical Psychology, 8,* 373–390.

Follingstad, D. R., Rutledge, L. L., Berg, B. J., Hause, E. S., & Polek, D. S. (1990). The role of emotional abuse in physically abusive relationships. *Journal of Family violence, 5,* 107–120.

Fontana, V. J. (1973). *Somewhere a child is crying: Maltreatment—causes and prevention*. New York: Macmillan.

Fortune, M. (1991). *Violence in the family*. Cleveland: Pilgrim.

Frank, P., & Golden, G. (1992). Blaming by naming: Battered women and the epidemic of co-dependence. *Social Work, 37,* 5–6.

Frankl, V. E. (1963). *Man's search for meaning: An introduction to logotherapy*. New York: Pocket Books.

Garbarino, J., Guttmann, E., & Seeley, J. W. (1989). *The psychologically battered child*. San Francisco: Jossey-Bass.

Gerzon, M. (1982). *A choice of heroes*. Boston: Houghton Mifflin.

Gilligan, C. (1982). *In a different voice*. Cambridge, MA: Harvard University Press.

Goldberg, L. (Producer), & Ruben, J. (Director). (1991). *Sleeping with the enemy* [Film]. Los Angeles: Twentieth Century Fox Film Corporation.

Gondolf, E. W. (1985). Anger and oppression in men who batter: Empiricist and feminist perspectives and their implications for research. *Victimology: An International Journal, 10,* 311–324.

Graham, Dee-L. R., Rawlings, E., & Rimini, N. (1988). Survivors of terror: Battered women, hostages, and the Stockholm syndrome. In K. Yllo & M. Bograd (Eds.), *Femenist perspectives on wife abuse* (pp. 217–233). Newbury Park, CA: Sage.

Hammond, N. (1989). Lesbian victims of relationship violence. *Women and Therapy, 8,* 89–105.

Hart, B. (1986). Lesbian battering: An examination. In K. Lobel (Ed.), *Naming the violence* (pp. 173–189). Seattle, WA: Seal.

Hart, S. N., Germain, R., & Brassard, M. R. (1987). The challenge: To better understand and combat the psychological maltreatment of children and youth. In M. R. Brassard, R. Germain, & S. N. Hart (Eds.), *Psychological maltreatment of children and youth* (pp. 3–24). New York: Pergamon.

Hearst, P., & Moscow, A. (1982). *Every secret thing*. New York: Doubleday.

Herman, J. L. (1992). *Trauma and recovery*. New York: Basic Books.

Hickox, A., & Furnell, J. R. G. (1989). Psychosocial and background factors in emotional abuse of children. *Child Care and Development, 15,* 227–240.

Hilberman, E., & Munson, K. (1977–1978). Sixty battered women. *Victimology: An International Journal, 2,* 460–467.

Hofeller, K. H. (1982). *Social, psychological, and situational factors in wife abuse.* CA: R and E Research Associates.

Hoffman, L. (1981). *Foundations of family therapy.* New York: Basic Books.

Hudson, W. W., & McIntosh, S. R. (1981). The assessment of spouse abuse: Two quantifiable dimensions. *Journal of Marriage and the Family, 43,* 873–885.

Jacoby, S. (1985, February). Emotional child abuse: The invisible plague. *Reader's Digest,* 86–90.

Janoff-Bulman, R. (1988). Victims of violence. In S. Fisher & J. Reason (Eds.), *Handbook of life stress, cognition and health* (pp. 101–113). New York: Wiley.

Jordan, J. V. (1991). The meaning of mutuality. In J. V. Jordan, A. G. Kaplan, J. B. Miller, I. P. Stiver, & J. L. Surrey, *Women's growth in connection* (pp. 81–96). New York: Guilford.

Junewicz, W. J. (1983). A protective posture toward emotional neglect and abuse. *Child Welfare, 62,* 243–252.

Kaplan, A. G. (1991). The "self-in-relation": Implications for depression in women. In J. V. Jordan, A. G. Kaplan, J. B. Miller, I. P. Stiver, & J. L. Surrey, *Women's growth in connection* (pp. 206–222). New York: Guilford.

Katchen, M. H., & Sakheim, D. K. (1992). Satanic beliefs and practices. In D. K. Sakheim & S. E. Devine (Eds.), *Out of darkness* (pp. 21–43). New York: Lexington Books.

Kohut, H. (1986). *The restoration of the self.* Madison, CT: International Universities Press.

Krugman, R. D., & Krugman, M. K. (1984). Emotional abuse in the classroom. *American Journal of Diseases of Children, 138,* 284–286.

Lawson, D. M. (1989). A family systems perspective on wife battering. *Journal of Mental Health Counseling, 11,* 359–374.

Lew, M. (1990). *Victims no longer.* New York: HarperCollins.

Lifton, R. J. (1961). *Thought reform and the psychology of totalism.* New York: Norton.

Loring, M., & Myers, D. (1991). *Differentiating emotionally abused women.* Unpublished manuscript.

Marshall, L. L. (1992). Development of the Severity of Violence Against Women scales. *Journal of Family Violence, 7,* 103–121.

Martin, D. (1976). *Battered wives.* New York: Pocket Books.

Mayeroff, M. (1971). *On caring.* New York: Harper & Row.

McCann, I. L., & Pearlman, L. A. (1990a). *Psychological trauma and the adult survivor.* New York: Brunner/Mazel.

McCann, I. L., & Pearlman, L. A. (1990b). Vicarious traumatization: A framework for understanding the psychological effects of working with victims. *Journal of Traumatic Stress, 3,* 131–149.

McCann, I. L., & Pearlman, L. A. (1992). Constructivist self-development theory: A theoretical framework for assessing and treating traumatized college students. *Journal of American College Health, 40,* 189–196.

Miller, A. (1981). *The drama of the gifted child.* New York: Basic Books.

Miller, J. B. (1986). *Toward a new psychology of women.* Boston: Beacon Press.

Murphy, C. M., & O'Leary, K. D. (1989). Psychological aggression predicts physical aggression in early marriage. *Journal of Consulting and Clinical Psychology, 57,* 579–582.

NiCarthy, G. (1986). *Getting free: A handbook for women in abusive relationships.* Seattle, WA: Seal.

Niles, D. (1992a). Posttrauma intervention strategies—part 1. *Advocate, 15,* 11.

Niles, D. (1992b, November). *Sexual Abuse and Post-Traumatic Stress Disorder.* Continuing education activity sponsored by the Georgia Psychological Association, Atlanta.

O'Neil, J. M. (1981). Patterns of gender role conflict and strain: Sexism and fear of femininity in men's lives. *Personnel and Guidance Journal, 60,* 203–210.

Partnoy, A. (1992). *Revenge of the apple.* Pittsburgh, PA: Cleis.

Patrick-Hoffman, P. (1982). *Psychological abuse of women by spouses and live-in lovers.* Unpublished doctoral dissertation, Union for Experimenting Colleges and Universities.

Pence, E. (1985). *Criminal justice response to domestic assault cases: A guide for policy development.* Duluth, MN: Domestic Abuse Intervention Program.

Pharr, S. (1986). Two workshops on homophobia. In K. Lobel (Ed.), *Naming the violence* (pp. 202–222). Seattle, WA: Seal.

Porterfield, K. (1989). *Violent voices: 12 steps to freedom from verbal and emotional abuse.* Deerfield Beach, FL: Health Communications, Inc.

Roberts, A. R. (1984). Crisis intervention with battered women. In A. R. Roberts (Ed.), *Battered women and their families* (pp. 65–83). New York: Springer.

Rohner, R. P., & Rohner, E. C. (1980). Antecedents and consequences of parental rejection: A theory of emotional abuse. *Child Abuse and Neglect, 4,* 189–198.

Rosenbaum, A., & O'Leary, K. D. (1986). The treatment of marital violence. In N. S. Jacobson & A. S. Gurman (Eds.), *Clinical handbook of marital therapy* (pp. 385–405). New York: Guilford.

Rounsaville, B. (1978). Theories in marital violence: Evidence from a study of battered women. *Victimology: An International Journal, 3,* 11–31.

Russell, D. E. (1982). *Rape in marriage.* New York: Collier.

Sakheim, D., & Devine, S. (1992). Bound by the boundaries: Therapy issues in work with individuals exposed to severe trauma. In D. K. Sakheim & S. E. Devine (Eds.), *Out of darkness* (pp. 279–293). New York: Lexington Books.

Scher, M., & Stevens, M. (1987). Men and violence. *Journal of Counseling and Development, 65,* 351–355.

Seligman, M. (1975). *Helplessness.* San Francisco: Freeman.

Sexton, A. (1966). *Live or die.* Boston: Houghton Mifflin.

Steinmetz, S. (1977). *The cycle of violence: Assertive, aggressive, and abusive family interaction.* New York: Praeger.

Straus, M. A. (1974). Leveling, civility, and violence in the family. *Journal of Marriage and the Family, 36,* 13–29.

Straus, M. A., Gelles, R. J., & Steinmetz, S. K. (1988). *Behind closed doors: Violence in the American family.* Newbury Park, CA: Sage.

Surrey, J. L. (1991a). The self-in-relation: A theory of women's development. In J. V. Jordan, A. G. Kaplan, J. B. Miller, I. P. Stiver, & J. L. Surrey (Eds.), *Women's growth in connection* (pp. 51–66). New York: Guilford.

Surrey, J. L. (1992b). Relationship and empowerment. In J. V. Jordan, A. G. Kaplan, J. B. Miller, I. P. Stiver, & J. L. Surrey (Eds.), *Women's growth in connection* (pp. 162–180). New York: Guilford.

Symonds, M. (1975). Victims of violence: Psychological effects and aftereffects. *American Journal of Psychoanalysis, 35*, 19–26.

Tolman, R. M. (1989). The development of a measure of psychological maltreatment of women by their male partners. *Violence and Victimology, 4*, 159–172.

Tolman, R. M. (1992). Psychological abuse of women. In R. T. Ammerman & M. Hersen (Eds.), *Assessment of family violence* (pp. 291–310). New York: Wiley.

van der Kolk, B. A. (1987). *Psychological trauma*. Washington, DC: American Psychiatric Press.

Waites, E. A. (1993). *Trauma and survival*. New York: Norton.

Walker, L. E. (1979). *The battered woman*. New York: Harper and Row.

Walker, L. E. (1983). Victimology and psychological perspectives of battered women. *Victimology: An International Journal, 8*, 82–104.

Walker, L. E. (1984). *The battered woman syndrome*. New York: Springer.

Walker, L. E. (1984b). Behavioral descriptions of violence. In L. E. Walker, *The battered woman syndrome*. New York: Springer.

Walker, L. E. (1988). The battered woman syndrome. In G. T. Hotaling, D. Finkelhor, J. T. Kirkpatrick, & M. A. Strauss (Eds.), *Family abuse and its consequences* (pp. 139–148). Newbury Park, CA: Sage.

Watts, D. L., & Courtois, C. A. (1981). Trends in the treatment of men who commit violence against women. *Personnel and Guidance Journal, 60*, 245–249.

Whiting, L. (1976). Defining emotional neglect. *Children Today, 5*, 2–5.

Wiehe, V. R., with Herring, T. (1991). *Perilous rivalry*. Lexington, MA: Lexington Books.

Index